# Dirty Jokes Your Mother Told Me

# Other Works by D.M. Engel

## Mystery

*Happy Birthday, You're Dead*

*The Case of the Filthy Vagina*

*Seymour Livingston: Poop Detective*

*The Girl with the Ugly Feet*

## Nonfiction

*Abraham Lincoln: Unbelievably Giant Asshole*

*California's Best Pruno*

## Science Fiction

*Star War*

*Cybertaint*

*Agoraphobe in Space*

## Erotica

*Meat the Obamas*

*The Episiotomist's Wife*

*The Episiotomist's Other Wife*

*Arched Back, Torn Groin*

*A Funeral to Remember*

# Dirty Jokes Your Mother Told Me
## A Collection of Short-Ass Fiction

## D.M. Engel

**VB**
Vagrant Books

Vagrant Books

Book design by D.M. Engel


Library of Congress Cataloging-in-Publication Data
Engel, D.M.
    Dirty jokes your mother told me: a collection of short-ass fiction / by D.M.
Engel.
        p. cm.
    ISBN-13: 978-0615592923
    ISBN-10: 0615592929

                                                    2012931242


                    10  9  8  7  6  5  4  3  2  1


                Printed in the United States of America

For all the filthy moms out there, who
have told me their dirty, dirty jokes.

# Contents

# Preface

When I began this literary journey, my book was entitled *Balls-Deep*, a hyper-sexual tell-all about my time as a self-made, high-end call girl for the Hollywood elite. However, I didn't like all of the hyphens, and so I decided to compile a collection of my short fiction instead. In the end it was the right decision, as I have never been a call girl.

In Steve Martin's *Pure Drivel*, he refers to his short fiction pieces as "little candy kisses, after-dinner mints to the big meal of literature…" If this is the case, then my pieces are Extra Strength Tylenol, taken the morning after an evening of bad decisions. Read one or two and they'll be sure to dispatch the rough edges of your day. Read them all at once and your liver may be destroyed. Enjoy.

Dirty Jokes Your Mother Told Me

# Footprints

Bob walked up to the gates of Heaven. He had just been hit by a car. George approached the gates from the Heaven side.

"How are you?" asked George.

"I'm fine," said Bob. "But something's been bothering me since I died a few moments ago. You see, it was almost like I was in a dream, and I was walking along the beach with the Lord. We were walking through all the different points in my life, and there were usually two sets of footprints. But I noticed that during the toughest times in my life, I only saw *one* set of footprints."

"That's because the Lord was carrying you," said George.

"You think?"

"It seems pretty clear to me," said George. "It's a

pretty common dream, and that's what most people tend to believe."

Another man appeared. His name was Jack. He had died an old man. "Yeah, I had one of those footprints dreams, but in mine, you know, there were two sets until it got to the tough points in my life. At those times, I only saw one footprint—a left foot—and a hole in the sand on either side."

"That sounds like the Lord was on crutches," said George. "But He still carried you."

"Really?" questioned Jack. "The Lord can get hurt?"

"Well," said George, "it's *your* dream. I mean…" George thought for a moment, and then just trailed off. "Anyway…"

Ken walked up. He had been hit in the head by a falling hammer on a construction sight. "What about *my* dream? Here it goes: Same footprints thing, two sets, all of that. But then, during the toughest points in my life, I only saw a set of *handprints*. What the hell is that?"

George spoke up. "That was when the Lord carried you while doing a handstand. I mean to say, he was walking on his hands."

"Really?" asked Ken. "That's…I mean…alright. Okay…whatever."

Next was Benny. He had just been eaten by a bear. "I had the same dream, two sets of footprints. But during the tough times there were two long lines in the sand and handprints on the outside."

"That was when the Lord carried you on his back while walking with his hands and dragging his feet," said George. The dead men all looked at each other. Then Benny spoke.

"His abs must look amazing."

"They do," said George. "You'll see."

Barry walked up. His wife had sent him a letter bomb. "I saw the footprints too, but in my toughest moments there weren't footprints at all, just a set of tire tracks."

"That's when He put you in His car and drove you," answered George.

"But these were small tracks," said Barry. "What kind of car does the Lord drive?"

"A Festiva," said George.

"They still make those?" asked Barry.

"Yes. In Europe," said George. "Over there they get more than seventy miles a gallon."

"That's incredible," said Jack.

"I had no idea they still made the Festiva," said Ken.

Having shared their stories, the men all stared down at the Earth one last time, thinking about how the Lord had carried each of them in their own way. It was quiet, and the expanse below was peaceful. Bob touched his index finger to the portion of his skull that had been caved in by the bumper of an '87 Buick Skylark. He thought back on his life and all of the beauty he had experienced. But one thing more than any other was stealing his thoughts, leaving him in disbelief.

"Seventy miles to the gallon?" he asked.

"Yep," said George. "Seventy miles to the fucking gallon."

# The Death of Time Travel

Derek had been hired right out of MIT by the Department of Defense. And, after a year-and-a-half of backbreaking work, he was finally putting the finishing touches on a time machine he called the Time Box. The Time Box was a clear Plexiglas cube with enough space for an average adult male to sit with his legs crossed. The upside of the Time Box was that the fabric of time had been conquered. Just a little over a century after human flight had been attained, man could now manipulate the past and future.

The downside of the Time Box was that in every case, the subject traveled back to just three minutes before their own conception and a mere five feet away from the actual event. Depressurization of the Time Box took three minutes, and so the traveler was forced to sit inside the clear cube against their will (presumably) and watch the final moments of the act that brought them into the world.

The nature of his work kept Derek secluded in the basement of an undisclosed government building. He had no contact with the outside world, save a few high-ranking military officials and a handful of quantum physicists. Yet Derek was hesitant to show even these people his findings. This was primarily due to the fact that he didn't want anyone to pass judgment on his work based solely on the first three minutes of the experiment. Thus, he was destined to run the trials on his own, which was nothing short of torture. A few keystrokes into the keyboard, a flash of blue light, and then the inevitable: His parents, undressed and intoxicated, writhing on an avocado-colored sofa in the apartment they had shared during their senior year at Stanford.

In those first minutes of the journey, Derek tried to review the incoming data stream from the onboard computer, but it was of little distraction. This wasn't a car crash that you had the liberty of looking away from. Rather, it was a car crash in which you were forced to identify the bodies. Science had cruelly declared that Derek must bear witness. His parents were too buried in one another's musk to notice their son, the physicist, essentially a stranger sitting next to them in a clear box. As the depressurization seal opened and Carol and Dennis climaxed, they were oblivious to their son's frantic departure.

Derek's obsession with the theory of special relativity was the cornerstone of his love of science. As an elementary student, he based all of his science fair projects on the work of Einstein, and even made a documentary on his favorite theoretical physicist for part of his capstone project at MIT. He never dreamed that he would someday be revered on Einstein's level, and yet this was the path he was currently clearing for himself. Having to watch his mother reach orgasm in order to earn his seat at the table of history's great scientists, however, somehow seemed unfair. *Why hasn't the future me come back to the present and fixed this disgusting problem?* he wondered. He knew that humans wouldn't have to watch their own parents copulate as a means of piercing the time-space continuum forever, but for now this was where the bar had been set. And so he trudged on, for science.

After several trips, Derek could easily determine how long it would be before the depressurization was complete by the rising position of his father's shoulders, the arching of his mother's back, and the building in volume of his father's unfortunately-placed phrase, "Deeper, Dennis!" It was during these pleasureless moments on the first few trial runs that Derek began noticing several exasperating changes. Everything would be the same—the sweat, the Jim Beam, the shaking glutes—with one or two distinct differences. Upon entering his fifth experiment, Derek's father's normally full scalp of sandy hair was completely gone, save a day's growth. During the sixth experiment, Dennis' hair was back—but now gray— while Carol's nails were three inches long, painted black and tearing deeply into Dennis' skin.

As the experiments persisted, the ripples in time's fabric extended into the community. Derek's high school baseball coach appeared shorter than he remembered, and the bathrooms at McDonald's were spotless. On the ninth trip, women's ears were all twice their normal size and the primary definition of the word "gay" was still "happy". By the eleventh trip to 1986, no one had teeth except for newborn babies and *Family Ties* had been canceled after only four seasons.

There was no way to verify whether or not these collective changes were applying themselves to Derek's present, as he was completely isolated. He couldn't bear the idea that he had reset humanity's code, yet he knew that his eyewitness accounts were frail onion paper compared to the steel girders he may have inadvertently erected. Could it be that he had stepped on a proverbial butterfly and sent nature into a tailspin? Or had other time travelers from further into the future successfully perfected his formula and traveled millions of years into the past, reconfiguring the human makeup from its very origins?

After his fifteenth trip, and after seeing Dennis and Carol's faces morphed into his own (but with neon blue sclerae and wolf paws for hands), he dismantled the Time Box with a flathead screwdriver and a hammer. He knew that the damage was now done, but he wasn't going to be party to it any longer. Pieces of the Time Box strewn across the small room he had called home for the last eighteen months, he stared at the door, wondering what he would find. Wolf paws? Enormous female ears? Neon eyes? He couldn't do anything about it now. Besides, he was hungry. And so he opened the door to a new world and headed for McDonald's. At least now they would probably have clean bathrooms.

# Go For It!™

Do you want it to happen? And by "it", I mean do you want *it* to happen? Are you ready for the success you've always dreamed of? Do you want to reach your personal mountaintop? Have you been to the mountaintop climbing store and bought all of the equipment necessary to climb to the top of that mountain? Have you purchased food rations for when the going gets tough? Are you ready to kick second place right in the asshole? If the answer is "Yes", my friend, then *Go For It!*™

That's right. *Go For It!*™ is what I call my foolproof guide to going for it and coming out on top. And there's just one way to do it: *Go For It!*™

That's all you have to do to beat the system and take control of your life! Ever wish you had more money? Ever wish you had a great girl with big breasts and lots of money? Ever wish you had friends who

9

loved how much money you had? Then *Go For It!*$^{TM}$ Get that money! Get those breasts!! Get those friends and *Go For It!*$^{TM}$

*Go For It!*$^{TM}$

How did I come up with this ground-breaking maxim for success? How did it all come about? Well, I'll tell you. Five years ago, I was thirty-one years old. I had just gotten a divorce from my second wife. My kids had been turned against me by their mothers because I couldn't pay child support, and I had developed what some people might consider an addiction to cocaine.

I woke up one morning with nothing. No money. No job. No girl. No clothes. I looked at myself in the mirror, hung over with an upper lip that was bloody from an evening of Colombian nose sugar. It was then that I realized what a disaster my life would become if I didn't establish a short, addictive catchphrase for capturing life and all of its wonder. And then it came to me: You can only get what you want in life when you *Go For It!*$^{TM}$ And so that's what I did! I went for it, and I got it, and now you can get it too!

This plan is simple in its design and easy to implement! Here's how it works!

Step 1: Figure out what you want to go for.

Step 2: *Go For It!*$^{TM}$

Step 3: You got it!

It's that simple! There's no small print in life, people. No reading between the lines or special skill set that winners like you and I need to have in order to get what we want. I got the car! I got the boat! I got the girl with breasts! And you can too! All you have to do is *Go For It!*[TM]

Do you want your father's respect? Your mother's love? Are you tired of watching your siblings snicker every time the word "disappointment" comes up in conversation? So was I, and now you have the power to do something about it! And do you know how?! Well, it won't be by not going for it! Hell no! Only when you dedicate your life to the full pursuit of going for it and acquire the stamina that going for it requires will you truly realize your full potential. So, are you ready?!

Then *Go For It!*[TM]

# The Crappy Pixar Movie

Long before critics saw the film, they predicted its downfall. "*Date Rape Danny*," wrote Roger Ebert, "is a computer-generated tale about a set of college-age male gonads separated from its frat boy body. This road opus is destined to be the production house's first big flop." Harsh words were coming down the pipe from all over Hollywood, and the flyover states voiced their distaste for weeks via AM radio call-in shows and nightly cable news broadcasts.

"I was raised to believe that date rape isn't a joke. If it were just a date, then sure, you could make a joke. But they're talking about date *rape*," insisted one irate caller into *Nancy Grace*. Nancy concurred.

"I don't care what people say to me, or what their belief system is. Date rape is wrong, even if it's rape on a date!"

Even New Yorkers—typically appreciative of a nuanced storyline that is dusted with backbiting irony—found a children's movie with the phrase "date rape" in the title hard to swallow. No one, it seemed, was willing to give Pixar the benefit of the doubt despite its unfettered batting average.

"*Danny* is a classic tale of a lost youth finding himself on the open American road," argued Ed Catmull, Pixar's president. "It is a cautionary tale, and Pixar refuses to shy away from sensitive social issues, even a tinderbox like date rape, simply because our motives are drawn into question."

Daniel, voiced by Casey Affleck, is a University of Michigan business major visiting Las Vegas with his fraternity brothers for March Madness. The night before they return to Ann Arbor, Daniel's wrongly-accused genitals—named Danny Balls and played by Mike Tyson—are severed from Daniel by several sorority sisters after Daniel is accused of not taking "no" for an answer with a women's studies major at UNLV. Set to a Randy Newman score, Danny Balls must hitchhike across the vast landscape of the Western United States to find Daniel, and along the way find himself.

Most everyone in Hollywood boycotted the premiere. However, a handful of critics and notable stars tied to Pixar attended the movie's opening night, and it was there that the juggernaut took hold. After the movie ended, Tom Hanks was one of the first to walk out of Mann's Chinese Theater, unable to speak as tears clouded his eyes and sobs filled his chest. Owen Wilson and Ellen DeGeneres left the theater holding hands, and Tim Allen hugged reporters and tourists who had stopped to take pictures. "Hold me," he repeated to everyone he met. "Hold me, hold me."

Almost immediately, glowing reviews began to flourish on the Internet. "Not in our lifetime," wrote Peter Travers, "has a film accomplished so much. It is possible that racism and alcohol abuse might actually be things of the past." Most other critics agreed, and the general discourse centered around which problems inherent to the human condition had been most securely quelled.

"I think I get Islam now," said Woody Allen while playing clarinet at the Carlyle Hotel in New York City.

"Bullshit," yelled a drunken Don Rickles from a nearby table. "It *all* makes fucking sense. I'll never do Vegas again. What's the point of insulting people? I want to *live*."

The truest testament to the film was that movie snobs and laymen alike agreed that no critique or rehashing could do the film justice; you simply had to see it for yourself. And so, I went to a viewing on a cold autumn afternoon in Manhattan. On the screen before me sat a wrinkled, weathered, drunken nut sack on the edge of a bed at the Luxor Hotel, holding a bottle of Jim Beam in one hand and a losing bet on Michigan versus Ohio State in the other. I watched as Danny Balls befriended Night Train, an old, bluesy armadillo played by Danny Glover, who lost his son in the first Iraq war and never forgave God. I cried as Danny Balls left a one-legged Muslim prostitute his winnings after finding Night Train dead with a needle in his arm. My heart broke as Randy Newman's "We All Walk Home Alone" played over a montage of

Danny Balls hitchhiking his way across the desert, his tender skin burning on the scorched asphalt. And in the end, as the audience stood up and applauded Danny Balls when he embraced Daniel in front of Angell Hall, I knew that we weren't merely cheering for Daniel's nut sack. We were cheering for humanity.

# My Dog's Blog

I was sitting in the terminal at LAX, browsing the Internet when I came across my dog's blog, *Incarceration Station: Tales From a Miserable Life*. It's all about his experience living with me, and it's pretty harsh. That night when I finally arrived home, I walked into the living room and there was Brian, my golden retriever, lying on the floor next to the computer, his tail beginning to wag.

"Hey there, Brian."

"What's up?" This caught me off guard. The blog had been a surprise, and yet for some reason I never expected him to talk. Shocked, I continued.

"I read your blog." He broke eye contact and his tail fell to the floor.

"That was supposed to be private," he said.

"But it was posted on the Internet, and it didn't require a password."

"I can't have a password. If I do, Google won't cache my site." At this point, Brian was teaching me things I didn't know about the Internet. He then tucked his head under his chest and began cleaning his genitals.

"Stop it," I said. "Who do you expect to read this? Half of your sentences begin with, 'Hey, have you ever noticed…?' Observational humor has been dead for a decade."

Brian turned to me and stood up. "Are you saying I'm not funny?" I didn't want to embarrass him, as his lack of vision wasn't the point. I changed the subject.

"I'm saying you're hurtful. These are reflections on our relationship. On my dating habits, my dental issues. You wrote about how I was afraid I would never make another woman laugh again. I told you that in confidence. It's embarrassing."

"But the stuff on you…no one even knows who you are."

"Right, but *I* know who I am, and *I* just read it."

"Right, but *you're* not my audience." This went on for a while. We didn't agree on Internet ethics, and so it was inevitable that we would come to an impasse. After another fifteen minutes of the back and forth, I said it was okay for him to leave up his post of my top ten terrible outfits. He agreed to take down the photo montage of me gaining fifty pounds after college, and the top six list of the best places where women had broken up with me.

Betrayal is a terrible die to have cast against you, especially when thrown by your best friend. I quietly walked upstairs and packed a clean set of clothes for the next morning's business trip, making the decision to let things go for now. It wasn't until I arrived at the airport that I discovered Brian's Twitter account linking to his Facebook page. He had reposted all of the words he had sworn he'd take down, and when I landed in Phoenix I considered cancelling my DSL and cutting him off from the outside world. But then I remembered the counter on his blog: No one was reading. And so, I decided to ensnare Brian with his mistaken sense of community, allowing him to sit in an existential room online with only himself for company. This seemed like punishment enough.

# The Asshole Family Reunion

The Asshole family reunion is held every July in Coal City, Illinois, a small farm town south of Chicago. Each summer the Assholes reunite at a local park, mend old ties, and for two days bask in the fellowship of extended family. This year was no different.

"What's up, Assholes?!" asked Dale Asshole, a brick mason from Joliet who brought his wife, Terri, and their three children. "Any of you pricks sober up yet?"

"Fuck you, Dale," said Jordan Asshole, Dale's first cousin and a recovering alcoholic. "You're a real Asshole!"

"Good one!" shot back Dale.

"How's your marriage counseling going?" asked Jordan. "Are you still seeing Samantha on the side?"

"Good and yes! I figured they cancel each other out," said Dale.

"It's great to be around a real fucking Asshole again, Dale," said Jordan.

"Same here," said Dale. Terri was within earshot, unwrapping turkey sandwiches and setting out the potato salad. Upon hearing her husband's comment, she put down a sandwich, looked up and spoke.

"Hey, Jordan? Ask Dale about how I maxed out our credit cards and gained forty pounds to spite his infidelity."

"She's a real Asshole," said Jordan. "Terri may not be blood, but she married into the right family!"

"How old is your oldest daughter now, Dale?" asked Robert, Jordan's father and the patriarch of the Assholes.

"Seventeen."

"Goddamn. She's like a hotter, perkier version of Terri. What I wouldn't give to be fifty years younger and on the right side of the law. Do you remember how I tried to nail Terri once when you were out of town on business? You know, before she let herself go?"

"Yes! What an Asshole!" said Dale.

"Yes, a real asshole," replied Terri, lighting up a cigarette as she mixed the potato salad.

"It's all water under the bridge now, of course," said Robert. The two cousins agreed, and they continued talking until Dale's sister, Cathy, walked over.

"Hey, Assholes! We're getting ready to rank all of the children in order of looks and then line them up to eat accordingly." Terri looked at Cathy. Cathy looked back.

"You don't have to be such an asshole. They're just kids," said Terri.

"It's never too early to turn your kids into real Assholes," snarked Cathy. "My married name may be Bernard, but I'm an Asshole through and through." Terri looked Cathy in the eye, stuck her entire right hand up to the wrist into Cathy's award-winning punch and then walked away. Robert saw this, shrugged his shoulders and double-dipped his plastic cup into the punch bowl, moistening his nicotine-stained fingers in the boozy liquid.

"It's too bad my brother isn't around to see how well your kids turned out, Dale," said Robert. "He never thought you'd amount to much...thought you'd die young from obesity like he did."

"Diabetes is a motherfucker," said Jordan.

"It's true," said Dale. "Obesity has killed more Assholes than I care to count."

Robert looked across the country road to the family cemetery. "Smoking. Booze. Shit diets. There are so many damn Assholes in the ground over there, simply because they couldn't get their act together. I miss those Assholes."

All of the men agreed. As they stared across the road at generations of Assholes, Terri pulled out of the park, drove past the cemetery and then out of sight. She had put their three children into the car and was driving them to her mother's, far away from those assholes for good. The men didn't know what to make of it. Probably just going above and beyond, they thought, doing whatever it takes to be a good ol', red-blooded Asshole.

# How to...Build a Deck

Having a deck is probably the greatest signifier of achieving the American dream next to owning an iPhone. And yet, so many times I have traveled to the homes of friends who are deckless. I'm not judging, but it's pathetic. Even though most of these people live in apartments, I'm quite certain they would find a way to build a deck off of their fire escape if they just had the know-how. And so, here are a few tips on how to build your own deck.

**Step 1: Find a place to have a deck.**
Make sure there isn't one already there. Get excited about the fact that you will soon have a deck. Think about the barbecues, family gatherings, and general deck fun you will have.

**Step 2: Consider what you want the deck to look like.**

Do you want it to connect to your house? Maybe you want it to look like the Millennium Falcon. Draw up some specs (a blueprint) and approximate the measurements. Don't worry about the math, as it usually works itself out.

**Step 3: Buy some wood and nails.**

True Value will have them, but they're pricey and have a limited selection, kind of like Radio Shack. Go to Home Depot or Lowe's instead. They are giant stores with all types of wood and nails. They also sell paper towels and laundry detergent, for some reason, in case you are out.

**Step 4: Bring the wood home and store it in your living room.**

If you are not strong enough, have someone else deliver the wood. Otherwise, have some self-respect and do it yourself. Store the lumber in your living room so you and your family can get to know the deck that you'll soon be spending so much time with. Think about what you might like to name the deck.

**Step 5: Stain the wood.**

Before *any* construction project, it is important to already have the lumber stained the proper color. Make sure you do this outside or in a ventilated area, or else you might stop breathing.

## Step 6: Build the deck.

Put the nails into the wood with a hammer or some other heavy, blunt object, like a meat tenderizer or a baseball bat. Use a saw or a sharp knife to cut the wood to approximate lengths.

## Step 7: Give the deck time to settle.

Nails need at least two weeks to "harden". In the meantime, think about Step 8.

## Step 8: Decorate your deck.

Add a picnic table, potted plants and a window chime. Use yellow paint to mark all areas of the deck that are dangerous. If you are a high society type who likes to be noticed, make a large banner that says "Deck" and hang it alongside your beautiful new space.

Enjoy your deck!

# Kanyedeus

Kanye lay in bed, dying. His skin was clammy, his eyes yellow and bloodshot. A fever had taken him over, and the only solace he found in his painful deterioration was in my visits. These visits were not as a confidant, however. Not at first. I wanted to see his body failing him with my own eyes.

Over the years his beats had eaten away at my very guts, at the spirit of my being. My own recordings were considered vapid and corny by critics. In my heart I knew their opinions to be true, and I hated Kanye for it. It was as if God had spited me with Kanye's consistent, almost divine musical vision. Relentless in his incorporation of strings, higher-pitched vocals and what seemed, in my estimation, a preoccupation with rock 'n' roll, his tracks were full, round and poppin'. And in time, as his life withered before me, so did my hateful revelry for this artistically triumphant rap artist. In an attempt to live, I sat at his bedside, scribing all of his thoughts, lyrics and beats, bringing samples to his room so that God might grant him enough waking hours to compose his own requiem.

"I don't understand! It's the first four bars of the *Night Court* theme song. The counts don't match up! This doesn't—"

"Hold on," he said. Kanye had pity on me, patiently waiting for me to learn. Weeks had gone by, and his breathing had grown shallow while his arms could barely hold up a piece of sheet music. He knew that I couldn't see what he was seeing, and he waited for the cloud of ignorance to blow away. "Take the first two bars. Then the first eight of the Motorhead snare riff."

"Wait…"

"Then add the last six bars from *Night Court*. Now double the speed. That's your eight."

From there the work sunk into my mind more quickly, but only because he was with me. We were breathing the same air, the carbon dioxide from his lungs dancing away from his doomed body and mixing with my own, swirling above us amongst the purified oxygen of his soundproof bedroom/beat laboratory.

"Now, read me back the lyrics."

"Larger livin' than the Cold Stone, Gangstra with the Ruby Red…"

"Cold Stone" was what Kanye called Biggie Smalls after a chance meeting shortly before Biggie's death. "Gangstra" was Jay-Z, a name he and Kanye shared for one another in order to incorporate the "r" from "Gangster" back into the black vernacular after a meaningful conversation the two shared regarding their mutual respect for Italian organized crime. "Ruby Red" was Beyoncé. He was combining the traditional shout outs and bragalicious black lyricism with white, twenty-first century irony. The lyrics became an explanation that his early life, career and soon-to-be tragic death were an international experiment in media exploitation.

"What's wrong?" he asked after handing me the final page of lyrics.

"Nothing. It's beautiful."

Then came the instruments.

"The trumpets."

"Yes?"

"Float them bitches over the jazz flute on an A."

The flutes, the trumpet, the sax from the eighties sitcom, the Motorhead. These instruments, beats and samples existed separately before the moments we were sharing. They had somehow remained asleep, dormant before my time at Kanye's bedside. But now, as he lay dying, they suddenly unified and burst forth like a primordial soup of contemporary black male identity.

I lined up the cues and levels. Kanye slept for an hour or so. Then, as if nothing had happened, he awoke again and another eleven or twelve hour session began just as quickly as it had ended. No food. No true sleep. He refused everything. The roots of my soul told me to pull my hand away, to not scribe for him, to not make him greater than he already was. This shrinking piece of me wanted to plunge the pen into his sunken chest, clog his throat with his own lyric sheets, strangle him with his X-Box controller. But to be a part of his music healed me, and in time the hatred shriveled into shame. Kanye was making me better than I could possibly be. Better than I would ever be again.

"You are my one true friend," he would say, over and over. I smiled. Kanye had betrayed everyone who had at one time or another protected his fragile self. The conservatives hated him for the Katrina charity fiasco. The Taylor Swift incident pissed off girls under the age of twenty-five, and *The Today Show* embarrassment, while somewhat understandable, had made him seem paranoid. After his tasteless Grammy presentation in what was later referred to as "white face", a large portion of the black community renounced their allegiance to him.

But these incidents had happened months and years ago. Now he was in his bed, alone. Alone, with me as his sole confessor. Me, a man who had come to his bedside hating him. A man who had brought to Kanye's home a decade of resentment. A man who had wanted nothing more than to fill that nigga's ass with lead. A man who now pitied a true artistic genius of our time and whose thoughts slowly became riddled with guilt and self-loathing.

Kanye's requiem neared completion. The tracks were laid down and Buchwald, his manager, came by to congratulate him and offer empty promises of recovery. I couldn't tell if it was for Kanye's benefit that Buchwald lied or his own, perhaps unable to face the loss of his greatest client.

My feigned friendship was all but nearing its coda as well. Though I had assumed my assistance would have made me whole again, upon leaving his deathbed for the last time I felt as hollow and alone as the flavorless albums I had dropped. I left Kanye on a Tuesday, his requiem complete and playing on his Bose iPod dock. The saxophone and classic base line from *Night Court* made me weep as I descended the grand staircase to his foyer. I never laid down another track, never pulled a sample, nor even free styled an insult again. The career I had spent a lifetime cultivating had come to an end. My own epitaph would say nothing of my personal accomplishments. Instead, it would boast that I had assisted the master in creating the most divine hip-hop dirge mankind has ever heard.

# Polite Phil

Everyone loved Polite Phil. He was a twig of a man whose security guard uniform hung from his elderly skeleton like wet toilet paper over a willow tree. The sheen of his balding head remained hidden under his gray cap as he held the doors open at Salem National Bank for each and every customer during his weekday shifts. In the thirty-seven years at his post, Polite Phil never missed an opportunity to say, "Have a nice day!"

"I can't believe how tall your boy is getting, Mrs. Dawson! You must be feeding him Miracle Grow!" he would remark, or, "Is that a new hair-do, Mrs. Kettle? You always seem to be on the edge of fashion!" There had never been any crime at Salem's largest bank, and so there was plenty of time for Polite Phil to learn all of his co-workers' birthdays while whittling miniature train sets for each of their children. But Polite Phil's greatest love was his customers, and he never failed to make each of them feel special. And this is precisely why, when three armed robbers approached the bank on a Tuesday morning, they were thrown off by Polite Phil.

"Good morning, boys!" he said, meeting them at the door. "A little warm for ski masks, isn't it?!" The men looked at each other. One of them turned to Polite Phil.

"Shut up, old man. Hit the floor."

"The customer's always right!" said Polite Phil, and he kneeled down and placed his face against the cold white tile. Polite Phil looked outside and noticed a driver wearing the same mask. "Your friend out there has a beautiful LeBaron! Is that an '89? My wife had the same model in powder blue! She's gone now..." The second robber approached Polite Phil, grabbed his holstered revolver and pistol-whipped the feeble guard on the side of his head with his own gun.

"AHH!!! Please...okee dokee!" said Polite Phil, not letting the deep, blinding pain get the best of his genteel spirits.

The men approached the counter, and within three minutes their duffle bags were full of cash. They walked briskly to the door, and Polite Phil, lying on the tile with blood pooling in his ear, couldn't let one more opportunity to brighten their day slip by.

"Don't spend it all in one place!" Just for that, the third man ran back into the bank and stomped on Polite Phil's back, breaking seven of his ribs.

"Creaahhhewww...sweet Betsy Jesus...please... come again!" As the men climbed into their Chrysler and drove away, Polite Phil thought to himself how proud he was that he had brightened the day of such strange young men. He thought of how he had stepped outside of his own comfort zone and helped three troubled boys, boys who were certainly at a low point in their own lives. He imagined that they would feel obliged to offer the same courtesy to the next citizens they encountered. For a moment, Polite Phil's pain melted away, his right temple ceased to throb, and a smile eased over his weathered face. And then his kidneys shut down.

# Flash Mob

Kyle felt like a total schmuck. His left eye was bandaged over, his right arm had been badly broken and his fingertips and arms were glazed over with cuts and bruises. And now, handcuffed to a hospital bed two weeks shy of his thirty-eighth birthday, he began to reevaluate things.

His wife had left with the kids two months earlier. Then he lost his maintenance job at the hospital—the hospital he was handcuffed to—where he had worked for fifteen years. His pink slip had been a move by the hospital to save money on rising Medicare costs, he had heard. In addition, his brother hadn't paid the three grand back that he'd borrowed, three grand that Kyle now desperately needed. His life was a geometry equation and Kyle was a C student, with each arc and angle falling into a precise formula seemingly defined to further screw up his life. But nothing compared to the flash mob.

Kyle had attempted to pick up the pieces at home after Brandy left, but he had failed miserably. Broken picture frames rested on the bedroom floor like empty shotgun casings, evidence of their violent purpose. Multi-colored Christmas lights lit up the front yard in February while the Christmas tree lights had burnt out from running on a twenty-four hour cycle. A pile of dishes in the sink, a bed that hadn't been made in seven weeks and a stack of empty pizza boxes on top of the stove rounded out the clichés that had become Kyle's life. But on a Saturday afternoon, as the snow collected in the driveway on top of the snow that had collected the weekend before, he sat in front of his computer, breathing heavily and in a panic. He had to reach out to someone. But who? To Kyle, Craigslist seemed like the obvious answer, and so he went there.

He clicked on "Community", and like a beacon in blue font, the letters on the first post stated: "Flash Mob, County General Hospital. 8PM TONITE!!!!" This was exactly what he had been looking for.

If he had clicked on the link, he would have realized that a flash mob was a spontaneous group of strangers who broke into dance and/or song at a predetermined time and place. He would have realized that everyone was supposed to show up having mastered choreography on YouTube that had been set to "Cherry Pie" by Warrant. Instead, Kyle thought it was going to be a group of picketers and people with pitchforks ready to have their voices heard, though he later admitted to himself and police that he had no idea why he envisioned pitchforks.

Kyle walked into Wal-Mart and purchased a three-foot length of log chain, a one-inch thick dowel rod and a pack of Trident. The dowel rod was to serve two purposes: The first was to hold a sign he intended to make that would say, "County General Makes Me Sick!" This was clever, he thought, because hospitals were a place to go when you *got* sick. Then, if and when things got hairy, the dowel rod would be used as a makeshift bat. The log chain was to be worn around his neck as a sign of dominance and possibly to fight off pitchforks, though in his scenario the pitchforks were on his side.

The gum was for his severe halitosis.

He climbed into his pick-up, slow to start from the lonely vapors left in its tank. He sat for a moment, thinking about what he might do. He didn't want to hurt anyone. This was too much. Kyle was a good man. A good man, but everything had been taken from him, and he realized that now it was time to say something, to stand up for himself, even if it meant holding up a sign and taking part in a flash mob. *How crazy could it get? Could people get hurt?* He asked these questions over and over, convincing himself that it would all be fine. *It's a building full of sick people, a place of physicians and educated human beings, of unionized staff with supposedly protected jobs and wages*, he thought. *I'll put the fear of God into them, but that'll be it.*

The plaza in front of the hospital was a public oasis of sorts: A field of cobblestone spotted with park benches, trees and bits of calculated sod. The snow had been cleared, and people sat drinking coffee and making phone calls in the brisk evening air. No one was there because they wanted to be, however. They *had* to be there. The staff was hammering a check, and the rest of the people were either sick or cared too much to not be visiting. This is how Kyle spotted the members of the flash mob: They looked like they *wanted* to be there. And that's when it hit him: These weren't protesters, eager to gather and unite. These were cowards waiting in corners of the plaza, virtually undetectable. These were liberals. These were the Medicare hustling sons of bitches who pulled his job out from under him. Destitute twenty- and thirty-somethings standing around and sitting on park benches, clad in stone-washed denim and frosted, teased out hair. *Jesus*, he thought, *it's no wonder why they need the government. Their clothes are a quarter-century old.*

Kyle saw some of them practicing what looked like choreography, though the steps were restrained, seemingly in an attempt to not draw attention. *This is a carefully calculated, left-wing beehive demanding government-funded health care*, he thought. Kyle knew now that he wasn't going to protest. He was going to kick some ass.

Suddenly, from speakers strategically planted in bushes throughout the plaza, a guitar riff that Kyle hadn't heard in over two decades flared through the air. Without warning, seventy-five men and women in Great White, Tesla and Warrant T-shirts began rushing to the center of the plaza. Kyle took his cue and ran as fast as he could in the same direction, swinging his dowel rod over his head and dropping innocent dancers from the back of the group like bowling pins. The participants assumed the screams and falls were somehow a part of the show, and continued their writhing in Keds and high tops, facing the hospital in staggered lines while Kyle took dancers' legs out from under them one by one. Why everyone seemed to be doing air guitar solos struck Kyle as odd, but there was too much adrenaline coursing through him to decipher this as a red flag. *Who the hell does a dance protest?* was the only discernable thought to pass through Kyle's mind.

Dancer after dancer hit the ground, the backs of their knees meeting the sweet spot Kyle had found on his dowel rod. After fifteen or so lay on the ground screaming, security concluded that Kyle hadn't been an original part of the choreography. They were soon on top of him, but not before he had broken up the flash mob.

# Madoff and Me

Bernie and I became friends back in the late nineties, those freewheeling days. You couldn't help but make money back then. "Sometimes I stand up from the toilet after my morning coffee, and there's a thousand bucks floating next to last night's dinner," I remember him joking. Things are different now for Bernie. And for me, I suppose. We don't see each other anymore, but when I think back, there were signs everywhere that he would become the man the world despises today.

"I found this program that lets you download music...*for free*," he once boasted. "I downloaded four hundred songs last night after *Leno*."

"You mean *stole*," I responded. When I said things like this, he always looked at me as if I said that I wanted to date his sister.

"It's music. Don't be such a faggot."

Once, on Seventy-Ninth Street and Lexington Avenue, we were waiting for a cab in the rain. Bernie spotted a mother with her two young children flagging down a taxi. Her four-year-old was wearing a Yankees cap, and Bernie quickly grabbed the cap and whipped it down the sidewalk when the mother wasn't looking.

"Ma'am, your child's hat…" he said to the woman, who took to screaming at her son long enough for Bernie to take the baby seat out of the cab, set it on the curb and pull me into the car.

"I love that shit! It makes me feel so alive!" he said, laughing as we pulled away, buckling his knees and clenching his fists.

"Was there really a baby in that pumpkin seat?" I asked.

"An *ugly* one," he said, shaking his head. He looked down at the floorboard, spotting a pink diaper bag next to his feet. Leaning back into the bench seat and looking out his window at the rain, he directed the cabbie. "The NASDAQ Building on Forty-Fourth Street. Step on it, Haji."

As time progressed, Bernie's delusions of grandeur heightened, and I have to say I worried about him.

"I'm thinking of acquiring the ocean." I explained to him that this would be impossible, and he gave me that date-your-sister look. Ruth worried about him too, and she was the one who told me what was going on at work.

"Shouldn't we tell someone?" I asked.

"He wants to buy the ocean and turn it into condos," she said. "I don't think prison is the best place for him." I didn't necessarily agree with her, but she was concerned for his health. I convinced myself that in time, maybe he could right his wrongs.

I tried sending him hints and jabs to wake him up to the destruction he was causing. I bought him a copy of *The Lorax* and wrote, "You" as the inscription. He thanked me for the book, saying it inspired him. Then he bought ten acres of timber in Upstate New York and chopped down every last tree himself. I took to pondering out loud, things like, "I wonder what prison food tastes like?" and, "Do you think betrayal is a distinctly human trait, or do all animals destroy one another?" and, "I wonder what the downside is for a person to take people's money and put it into a Chase savings account rather than investing it in the market like they promised?"

"I never know what the fuck you're talking about." This was always what he said.

I was there when he told his sons. Mark and Andrew just looked at him, speechless, for an hour. Then they turned to me.

"Don't look at me," I said, pointing my thumb at Bernie and shaking my head. "I don't understand any of it, except that he is totally fucked." With this his sons asked me to leave, and after that night the four of us never spoke again.

Now, years later, I often sit alone in Central Park on the bench where he used to throw rocks at children, and I mourn my own responsibility to all those people who believed in him. I could have saved the teachers' pensions, the construction workers' retirements, Kevin Bacon's third boat money. And now, each time a friend of mine tries to illegally download pirated music, scam a mother of two out of a cab, or buy an ocean, I don't shrink back from their disapproving looks. No, now I speak my mind and let them know that if they ever try to steal $65 billion, I will turn them in.

# All Men Cheat

Listen, ladies. I have to tell you something. You may think you have your man figured out, but let me ask you this: Where is he right now? Fixing the furnace? Grouting the bathroom tile? Right. Listen to me good: He's cheating on you.

I don't mean, "He's cheating on you" as in, "He's got someone on the side that he's going to take riverboat gambling this weekend." No, what I'm saying is, he's cheating on you *right now*, in the bathroom while he's sitting on the toilet. There could be another woman in there, and let's just say what they might be doing wouldn't make it onto your Christmas card.

Men don't need much time or space to cheat, and so you can never be too careful. Have you ever asked your husband to take out the trash? Then you messed up, because that's plenty of time right there. Not to mention the fact that a trash can contains more than enough room for two people to bring a good marriage to a screeching halt. Have you ever run into the house to grab one last thing before the two of you left for the weekend? Well then, you've given your husband carte blanche to backseat-pork any slut in the entire neighborhood.

Have you ever asked him to get something out of the garage? You wouldn't believe it, but this is where ninety percent of men are unfaithful to their wives. That's right, right next to the workbench and your kids' fishing poles. I knew a guy that hid women in his cat's litter box. The stink from the cat poop covered up the sex smell perfectly. If you look, there are at least three or four women somewhere in your house at all times; two if you have an apartment.

Real women know this. My wife doesn't let me stand more than two feet away from her. Ever. She plans her showers for the two times a day when I poop. In fact, she's watching me write this right now. And while this may seem extreme, I can tell you this: I have never cheated on her. But if she ever turned her back for one second to check on the kids or fold the laundry, there's a little blonde number stuffed under the sink that's ready to give me the old what for.

All I'm saying is, don't take for granted the fact that he's in the kitchen making dinner. Can you see him? If you can't, then you might as well be asking him to mess around.

# Smoking Hot Couple Fuck One Another to Death

Malibu, CA—A sculpted, bronzed and totally smoking hot couple was found dead in a condominium complex early Saturday morning, apparently the victims of sexing one another to death. The violent coitus had by victims Candice Abraham and Ron Colgate was reportedly heard and smelled by dozens of people within a two-block radius over several days. "I've been on the force for twenty-five years, and I've never seen anything like this," said Detective James Ramsfield of the Malibu Police Department. "The smell in there is overpowering…and totally hot."

It was a crowded crime scene, as everyone involved in the investigation wanted to get a firsthand look at the bodies. "It's so fucking sexy," said Officer Chaz Decker. He added, "They were in the crab position, which is my favorite." He stated that there were hundreds of soiled condoms and a case of empty lubricant bottles, both oil- and water-based. "It's a good thing no one actually *saw* them having sex, or else we might be looking at a higher body count."

Michael Ellis, the Malibu Coroner, said that though the cause of death was still unofficial, it was most likely a combination of severe dehydration, blood loss from intense genital trauma, and, as he put it, "unbearable fucking hotness."

Residents of the Luxton Towers apartment complex first reported hearing the couple's single, prolonged session in the early evening on Tuesday. When neighbors awoke Wednesday morning to similar but more intense sounds, they thought nothing of it. "They're a new couple," said one resident. "That's what happens."

It wasn't until Thursday morning that the couple's respective places of employment became concerned and began to inquire as to their whereabouts. Mr. Colgate's brother said he never filled out a missing persons report because he came by the apartment on several occasions, but had to leave due to his "erection from the jungle sounds coming out of that condo."

By Friday, neighbors and passers-by had become concerned. "The noise was constant and unbearable," said Luxton Towers resident, Harold Weaver. "I called the police once the moans and yells turned into constant screaming, but the authorities did nothing." Added Mr. Weaver's wife, Gladys, "Maybe if they drank more water. Ate some bananas. I don't know. It's just so senseless…and so fucking hot."

# The Giving Tree*

Once there was a tree…

***

and she loved a little boy.

***

And every day the boy would come

***

and he would gather her leaves

***

and make them into crowns and play king of the forest.

*Each "***" indicates a new page in the original book by Shel Silverstein.

46

\*\*\*

He would climb her trunk

\*\*\*

and swing from her branches

\*\*\*

and eat apples.

\*\*\*

And he would play hide-and-go-seek. With a tree.

\*\*\*

And when he was tired, he would sleep in her shade.

\*\*\*

And the boy loved the tree…

\*\*\*

very much. So much that he vandalized it by carving his initials into it with a knife.

\*\*\*

And the tree was happy. The tree had been abused as a child, so the vandalism made her feel loved.

\*\*\*

But time went by.

\*\*\*

And the boy grew older. And the boy had sex with a few girls next to the tree, which annoyed the tree. The boy even carved one girl's name into the tree, which the tree found hurtful.

\*\*\*

And the tree was often alone. Some people find this sad, but after all, it was a fucking tree.

\*\*\*

Then one day the boy came to the tree and the tree said, "Come, Boy, come and climb up my trunk and swing from my branches and eat apples and play in my shade and be happy."

"I am too big to climb and play," said the boy. In all fairness, he was. He looked to be about twenty, and it was time to grow up. "I want to buy things and have fun. I want some money. Can you give me some money?"

"I'm sorry," said the tree, "but I have no money." *I'm a fucking tree*, thought the tree. "I have only leaves and apples. Take my apples, Boy, and sell them in the city. Then you will have money and you will be happy."

\*\*\*

The boy knew he wouldn't get much for the apples, but he was out of options. He was apparently above getting a job. And so the boy climbed up the tree and gathered her apples and carried them away. Every goddamn apple she had. And the tree was happy.

\*\*\*

But the boy stayed away for a long time…and the tree was sad. Probably because the tree had never been valued in a relationship before. And then one day the boy came back and the tree shook with joy and she said, "Come, Boy, climb up my trunk and swing from my branches and be happy." The fact that the tree was shaking made it look desperate to the boy, but the boy needed something, and so he looked past it.

\*\*\*

"I am too busy to climb trees," said the boy. He was pushing forty, and so the very idea of climbing trees seemed nothing short of retarded. But anyway, he needed lumber. "I want a house to keep me warm," he said. "I want a wife and I want children, and so I need a house. Can you give me a house?"

*What the fuck?!* thought the tree, but she wasn't kidding herself. This was a co-dependent relationship, and if she were going to feel fulfilled, she would have to do something crazy. "I have no house," said the tree. "The forest is my house," she added sarcastically, stopping herself from suggesting that he ask someone who wasn't rooted to the ground. "But you may cut off my branches and build a house. Then you will be happy."

\*\*\*

And so (surprise!) the boy cut off her branches and carried them away to build his house. He carried them away to build, it would seem, the smallest house anyone has ever built.

\*\*\*

And the tree was happy. The tree felt like a martyr, which was the only thing left in life that brought her any satisfaction.

\*\*\*

But the boy stayed away for a long time. A helluva long time, because the next time he showed up he was easily in his sixties. And when he came back, the tree was so happy she could hardly speak. "Come, Boy," she whispered, "come and play."

"I am too old and sad to play," said the boy. *You idiot,*

he thought. M*y wife died of cancer and my kids hate me for being an alcoholic*. Then he continued. "I want a boat that will take me far away from here. Can you give me a boat?"

\*\*\*

The tree let out a deep, passive-aggressive sigh. Then she said, "Cut down my trunk and make a boat. Then you can sail away…and be happy." Obviously the tree was missing the point. The boy wasn't ever going to be happy. But she loved being put upon, and she had raised the boy to treat her like shit.

\*\*\*

And so the boy cut down her trunk

\*\*\*

and made a boat and sailed away.

\*\*\*

And the tree was happy…

\*\*\*

but not really.

\*\*\*

And after a long time the boy came back again. He was impossibly old and appeared to be wearing some type of unitard. The tree was hurt by the boy's decades of neglect, but got off on feeling like a victim to such an extent that all she could say was, "I am sorry, Boy, but I have nothing left to give you—"

\*\*\*

"My apples are gone," she added. The boy wasn't interested. She had never taught him to think of anyone but himself, so he didn't.

"My teeth are too weak for apples," said the boy. This was clearly bullshit, as the boy didn't appear to have a single tooth in his head.

"My branches are gone," said the tree. "You cannot swing on them—"

*No shit. I took them*, thought the boy. He dug his index fingernail into his thumb and said, "I am too old to swing on branches."

"My trunk is gone," said the tree. "You cannot climb—"

"I am too tired to climb," said the boy, cutting her off. *When is this bitch going to SHUT UP? I just want to sit down and take my Coumadin.*

"I am sorry," sighed the tree, in the way that ate through the boy's skin. "I wish that I could give you something…but I have nothing left. I am just an old stump. I am sorry…"

\*\*\*

If it was an apology she wanted, she wasn't going to get it. The boy knew what he had done, but he didn't respect the tree enough to apologize. Instead he attempted to change the subject back to what he was after. "I don't need very much now," said the boy, "just a quiet place to sit and rest. I am very tired."

"Well," said the tree, straightening herself up as much as she could, "well, an old stump *is* good for sitting and resting. Come, Boy, sit down. Sit down and rest."

\*\*\*

And the boy did. And then he shit himself.

\*\*\*

And the tree was happy.

\*\*\*

The End

# Babies Raising Babies

Paul and Dorna arrived home from the hospital with their twin boys, Arliss and Artem. Both parents were exhausted, and Paul had complained on the way home about how it was Dorna's turn to change the boys' diapers.

"I changed them, like, sixteen times at the hospital," he said.

"I changed them, like, nineteen or twenty," said Dorna.

"Did not."

"Did too." It went on like this, as it often does, in cases of babies raising babies. Paul finally got his way after pulling Dorna's hair, but Dorna then retaliated by bending Paul's finger back and breaking his favorite markers. Both ended up crying in separate corners of the living room, only to calm down ten minutes later and construct building block castles together on the coffee table. Then Paul kicked over the building blocks for no apparent reason, sending Dorna into a fit. The twins screamed from their bouncy seats on the kitchen counter.

"Drink, baby," said Dorna. She knew how to feed herself, but making the twins eat was beyond her threshold of understanding. She placed the plastic milk jug up to Arliss' mouth, fully expecting the newborn to reach for it and tip it up to his own lips. "It's milk, get it?" When he didn't respond, she pressed the jug gently against Arliss' face, hoping that this would send the message. It didn't, and so she threw the jug across the kitchen.

Paul wasn't doing much better. The dental floss he was using to secure Artem's diaper was irritating the baby's skin, and the toast he had attempted to make for the twins' breakfast wasn't getting cooked because he couldn't figure out how to plug in the toaster. It was hopeless.

Eventually, the babies were taken away, but Paul and Dorna didn't seem to mind.

"Now we have more time to build forts with our couch pillows," Paul said to Dorna reassuringly.

"Yeah," she said, "we would have gotten bored with them anyway."

# Newspaper

Mary and Joe stood at the edge of their driveway with their Portuguese water dog, Troy. This was the ritual: Get the paper, make breakfast, feed Troy. But there was a crimp in the system, and lately they didn't know what to make of their new paperboy. Joe hadn't gotten up early enough to spot him, but he assumed he was dealing with a kid who had an aversion to grass and front porches, as the paper usually arrived as a casualty of a weak-wristed throw, often landing a foot short of the curb.

This wasn't the meat of the issue, however. They had gotten used to retrieving tread mark-riddled editions of *The New York Times* from the street, but lately the deliveries had taken a turn for the worse. Occasionally, bite marks had found their way onto the edges of the paper. After a few weeks, certain sections had been ripped apart altogether, then oddly placed back in order and neatly curled into an unassuming role. Joe would have been able to deal with simple vandalism, but the fact that he was tricked into carrying the periodical into the house and discovering the crime while sitting on his own couch was enough to make him see red.

"Why do they *roll it up?!*" he would scream at Mary. "This makes me want to *kill* someone!"

"I don't know, Joe," she would say, having already moved on to aspects of the day she could control. "Did you pick up Troy's new dog food? You said you would do it ages ago. His stomach can't handle the stuff he's on, and for some reason he smells like cigarettes. Have you been smoking again?"

Joe had, but he ignored this and just looked at Troy. Troy looked back, past the black curls of his muzzle as if to say, "I need that new food. My poop looks like gravy. Help me."

Joe ignored this, too. He didn't care. Troy was Mary's dog anyway, and she had taken to coddling him like a child. Joe had grown up with hunting dogs, and his father's beagles and Labradors had been treated like firearms to be maintained and respected, not pets to get weepy over. *If she makes me take that dog to the vet for a runny nose one more time I am going to scream*, he thought. Just then, a droplet of moisture fell from Troy's snout. *Fuck*, he thought. Joe looked down at the paper, remembering again the handfuls of shredded business section he now had to throw away.

"FUCK!"

Joe had called the *Times* office and offered a barrage of complaints, but it hadn't solved anything.

Weeks went by. New paperboys came and went, and it appeared as if each one had been fired in succession for their vandalism, but only after teaching their apprentice how to properly destroy the newspaper. It simply never stopped.

Months passed. Mary hadn't looked at the paper in ages, but Joe continued to read it on principle. "No asshole paperboy is going to get in the way of my travel section. Fuck HIM." But the recent addition of cigarette burns to the eyes of faces in the newspaper was more than Joe could take. *This dickface is raising the bar*, he thought, and Joe hadn't so much as laid an eye on the underage teen.

And so he decided to stake out what he assumed would be some sixteen-year-old punk on his bike route before school. He set his alarm for five o'clock, and when the ringer went off he threw on his brown robe, poured a thermos full of coffee and loaded his paintball gun with two hundred rounds. He hesitated before applying black grease paint under his eyes, staring at his face in the bathroom mirror. *Jesus*, he thought, *is this too much?* A thousand answers could have crept into his mind and steered his destiny, like *You're thirty-five*, or *Mary will kill you*, or *You might get arrested for endangering the life of a child*. Instead, some vague notion about defending what is yours climbed into his brain and took hold.

Joe quickly smeared the paint under is eyes, walked outside with his thermos and his gun and hid behind the bushes beneath his bedroom window like an animal. He had been waiting for over an hour when slowly, as the sun pierced the horizon, a boy on an orange Huffy appeared in a red hooded sweatshirt. He couldn't have been more than fourteen, but Joe didn't care. He was going to shoot him square in the asshole.

The boy reached into the blue canvas satchel that rested on the handlebars of his bike. With his right arm he whipped the roll behind his back, squarely hitting the front door and landing on the porch. Joe's trigger finger relaxed out of confusion, and he stood up in his robe from behind the dew soaked bushes as the boy rode away.

Almost instantly, Troy came running from the doggy door at the back of the house and towards the front porch. Joe crouched back down as Troy trotted up to the paper, carried it to the street, peeled the rubber band off with his teeth and paws and carefully unrolled the *Times* until he reached the business section. He picked up section B with his canines, and Joe could see Troy tightening his jaws just before the dog shredded every last piece of his owner's favorite pages. He then surgically placed the paper back into its original form and rolled it up, using his nails, nose and tongue to replace the rubber band.

Troy then stood up on his hind legs, pulled a Zippo lighter and Joe's pack of Camels out of his fur and lit a cigarette. He stood there for several moments, taking long, flavorful breaths, eyeballing the Camel as it rested between two of his toes. Drag after drag went into his lungs until he was almost down to the filter. It was then that Troy burnt the eyes out of two faces on the rolled up newsprint, gray smoke lifting into the air from the hot orange embers. Then he dropped the paper where he stood, gagged from the smoke in his chest and shook his body wildly on all fours. Panting all the way back to the kitchen, he flicked the butt into the neighbor's yard. Joe stood behind the waste-high bush, thermos in one hand and paintball gun in the other. He dropped them both and walked to his truck. Hearing the engine start, Mary opened the bedroom window.

"Joe?" she asked, "Where are you going?" Joe didn't look at her, but simply rolled down his window as he pulled out of the driveway.

"I'm gonna go and get Troy's new dog food."

# Michael Collins Forced to Tell Students He Didn't Walk on the Moon

MONTGOMERY, AL—While speaking with second grade students yesterday at Jefferson Elementary about being a member of the first moon landing in 1969, former astronaut Michael Collins was forced to admit to students that he "hadn't actually walked on the moon." As students looked at him in confusion, he added, "Neil (Armstrong) and Buzz (Aldrin) walked on the moon to collect rocks. It was my job to man the Apollo 11 capsule while they were gone."

"Why?" asked Tim Kestler, a second grader in Mrs. Jones' class. "Were they better astronauts?"

Seven-year-old Rick Bilkins added, "Yeah, didn't you get good grades?" After a series of pointed questions, Mr. Collins replied, "No, I was just as good as they were." A few uncomfortable moments later he added, "In fact, I was the best at flying the spacecraft. That's why I stayed on board."

"I think I'd still rather walk on the moon," said Chad Donohue, eight. Mrs. Jones concurred. "It would have been torture to see what was going on outside and have to sit in that module," she said.

After making a joke about being able to relax and eat dried ice cream and drink Tang while the other two astronauts did all the work, Mr. Collins did find one converter. "That sounds good," said Jimmy Portis, an obese eight-year-old with curly red hair. "I would have stayed and eaten, too."

# Your Mom

Your mom called me today. She wanted my proctologist's phone number. Also, she had a question about her bad credit, her recent driver's license suspension, and my opinion on zone defense. She wanted me to tell you that you don't call her enough and that her UTI is gone. She also wanted to know if she could borrow five bucks for some toothpaste.

Call your mom. Her breath stinks and she's pathetic.

# Brice Kepple Will Teach You Guitar

There are few certainties in life: Death, taxes, the love of your mother. Socrates himself said the only thing he knew was nothing at all. But he was a fool. Though not in abundance, there *are* powerful absolutes in life; one simply needs to know where to search. No one should, in old age, look back upon the landscape of their life with inept and cloudy eyes, uncertain what they might have clung to had they only sought the truth. Therefore, my friends, I offer a power and skill set that few master, a craft that will lead God to approach with merciful eyes on your judgment day, a dynamism that will humble your greatest critics and crush your own self-doubt. In the disorienting mist of our fleeting lives, know this one, rock solid truth: Brice Kepple will teach you guitar.

Do you want to learn sliding scales? Minor chord inversions? Or do you simply wish to glean your favorite Beatles tune from a repetition of basic, open chords? It makes no difference, for no goal of my students is too shortsighted or too far from reach. Thousands have I ingratiated with my knowledge and power. Thousands have I sent back into the world, brave and impervious to the violent pain that comes from not knowing the dominant seventh chord.

Exodus 14:31 says, "And then the Israelites saw the great power the Lord displayed against the Egyptians, and the people feared the Lord and put their trust in Him and in Moses, His servant." This is the trust of which I speak: Confide in me as you would in God, and I will deliver delicious licks just as Moses delivered his people from the desert.

I will teach you rock guitar. Have you ever had the desire to rock? Does your love of this African-American inspired genre transcend an appreciation for Spandex, flannel and chest hair? Do you see the electric guitar as both an engine for social change and the ultimate pussy magnet? Then I will fall scales from your eyes with the inherent goodness and salvation of rock 'n' roll.

I will teach you blues guitar. Have you ever been dumped by your significant other? Has the Man ever forced you to work from sundown 'til the break of day, all the while your woman was at home, sharing her sugar love with your best friend? You will learn to express emotions through your fingers with the dexterity of Willie Dixon and the soul of Muddy Waters. Do you believe that achieving success as a musician requires a hopeless addiction to heroin and seventeen illegitimate children? Then blues guitar is for you.

There are some things that I will not teach you.

I will not teach you about love. While Eddie Van Halen's breakneck chord progression and slippery, seductive fingering up the neck of his '75 Stratocaster qualifies him as a legitimate force in the study of the female body, this cannot be taught. The scales? Yes, I can teach you the scales. I *will* teach you the scales. But can I teach you the boundless joy you will one day experience from a lover's touch? The transcendental arousal that will set your loins aflame merely from your lady friend's scent? No, I cannot teach you these things.

I cannot teach you how to come to terms with the inevitability of death. I have neither the knowledge nor the time to delve into your psyche and unlock the human ability to overcome grief and sorrow. I only have the tools to teach you guitar.

I also cannot teach you to sing. I have no background in vocal technique.

Though I have just listed numerous subjects that I will not teach you, please keep in mind that I will teach you guitar. The lessons will be strenuous. We will start with basic terminology. This is not negotiable. I will then illustrate proper physical contact with the guitar and placement of the hands and digits. Then we will move on to open chords.

The distance you travel with my unbridled talent entirely rests upon your will. Remember, Psalm 27:3 says, "Though an army besiege me, my heart will not fear; though war break out against me, even then will I be confident." And like the sure-footedness of the Lord, my skill set is loving and good. But it is more than God's precious love. It is tantric in its spirituality, washing over your body and soul, enveloping your heart and guiding your hands until, after months of constant, enduring penetration into your until-now untapped potential, there will be an explosive epiphany as my warm, lubricating talent washes over you, into your eyes, nose and throat, filling your body cavity with my salty teachings.

Keep in mind that I also have classes for advanced students. But regardless, one truth remains: In this incendiary world of uncertainty and doubt, I will bear the burden of your now untalented fingers, your clumsy hands, your empty soul. And, save the coming of our Lord Jesus Christ on His winged horse to reclaim us once again and deliver us to Paradise, Brice Kepple will teach you guitar.

# How to...Sweep the Leg

America has a long, rich heritage of youth violence. For decades we have asked ourselves who is at fault: Parents? Poverty? A lack of education? As we have learned from science-based cable news studies, these answers are stupid, and Hollywood is singularly to blame. Because life will always imitate art, we must try and utilize film to guide children away from the TEC-9 and towards an ass beating that everyone can walk away from.

Fortunately, there are a few clear guideposts to such behavior in the American movie canon. Quite possibly the best example can be found in the 1984 film, *The Karate Kid*. And so, since there are so many adolescents out there who feel the need to cloak their insecurity and pent-up homoeroticism in violence, here is a sure-fire, step-by-step method to being a dick without anyone really getting hurt.

**Step 1: Seek out a male role model who will abuse you.**

In this day and age, this is tougher than it sounds. However, if you are going to karate-kick some ass on a constant basis and remain unfettered by guilt, you will need a catalyst strong enough to help you override the nature of human compassion. Alcoholics will do just fine, as well as most high school football coaches and police officers. These adult males were themselves neglected and/or emotionally scarred as young people, and so they are the most likely candidates in terms of giving you what you need.

**Step 2: Hone your anger in the form of a leg-sweeping skill set.**

While many contact sports might be considered sufficient, the martial arts are the clearest path to sweeping the leg. They offer a complete ass-kicking skill set while enabling a small fraction of dicks to avoid the ethics of the art form. This is you. Practice your craft diligently, and typically with someone else's leg in mind. Is there a punk at school whose confidence you find emasculating? Simply picture him as a leg in a karate gi and sweep him.

**Step 3: Find a leg to be swept.**

There should be no shortage of these. Now that you have dedicated your existence to martial arts for the last three weeks to ten years, it is time to observe or manufacture a justification for sweeping someone's leg. Is the leg attached to a person who disrespected you by not properly accepting a beating? Does the person stir in you homosexual impulses that you are unable to emotionally address? Does the person not drive a Camero? Once you have found the outsider who doesn't have enough money to buy Jordache Jeans, you can move on to Step 4.

### Step 4: Publicly humiliate the innocent person out of nowhere.

Malls and high school hallways work best. This is where all social classes hang out, and at some point you will find the opportunity to dump a Slurpee on the head of a deserving nobody while on your way to Abercrombie. Plus, the girl who dates you out of fear will either be more attracted to you, or dump you for the victim. The latter will give you an even bigger reason to sweep the leg.

### Step 5: Take offense to a public rebuke by the victim.

Allow the victim to check your shoulder or make a witty comeback to a comment you made about their lack of hair care product usage. Then inform them publicly that you intend to sweep their leg. Demonstrate a series of leg-sweeping moves in front of the crowd. This will work as a teaser for the audience, and allow you to more fully visualize the future leg sweeping.

### Step 6: Plan the event!

Choose an environment that is both public and controlled. Abandoned parking lots work well, as large crowds can be formed. An organized martial arts tournament is ideal, as it allows you to be surrounded by potentially abusive male role models and like-minded peers.

## Step 7: Sweep the Leg.

Now it is time for the leg sweeping. If you have followed the previous steps, you should be able to properly kick some ass. Upon completion, inform the victim that their leg has been swept. Next, seek out praise from your male role model, and discuss with your peers who you intend to cheat on your girlfriend with at the lake party.

You did it, Goju master!

# I Think I'm in Love

I met someone the other day, and I think I'm in love. Her name is Alice. She has beautiful, long auburn hair, green eyes and huge knockers. She makes me laugh, but not so much that I'm intimidated by her sense of humor. And she didn't go to college, which means I never have to feel like she knows more than me. Her dad wasn't around when she was a kid, and her last boyfriend used to yell at her all the time, so she pretty much goes out of her way to not cause any problems. Also, she can suck the chrome off of a trailer hitch.

I think it's really love this time.

# Q and A: Charlie McCarthy

*Charlie McCarthy is arguably the most recognizable and prolific ventriloquist doll of the twentieth century. When most Americans were struggling through the Great Depression, Edgar Bergen and McCarthy owned the radio waves.* The Bergen and McCarthy Show *began in 1937 and soon became the number one program on radio. Stars like Clark Gable and Mae West lined up to feed off of McCarthy's energy for three decades. He was even engaged to Marilyn Monroe until it was learned that he could not submit to a blood test.*

*Dejected, McCarthy began seeking out other creative avenues within entertainment while still working with Bergen. He started his horror career in 1959 on an episode of* The Twilight Zone, *and over the years has earned his stripes as both an actor and consultant. Recently, Carl Weathers sat down with McCarthy to discuss his pain over Marilyn, being godfather to Rod Serling's daughter, and why he's known more for scaring children than for his musical numbers during the golden age of radio.*

Carl Weathers: A lot of controversy surrounded your entrance into the spotlight back in the mid-to-late thirties. Why is that?

Charlie McCarthy: I think that there were a lot of people who had a serious problem with a ventriloquist doll making more money than they were. Remember, this was the Depression. No one was making money, and I was pulling in one hundred dollars a week. It was sensational. Then again, my detractors were certainly in the vast minority. You can't have a number one radio show for decades and have the masses loathing you at the same time. Well, these days you can… reality shows and such. But back then radio was the format, and if you didn't like someone you just phoned your congressman (laughing). People actually used to call their representatives to get people off the air. Señor Wences and Pedro weren't completely blacklisted, but they did suffer from audience backlash. Of course, they were communists.

CW: What led to your role in *The Twilight Zone* in the late fifties?

CM: Probably a lot like when you did *The Hostage Tower* back in the seventies. I had played the mischievous, jovial little—

CW: I wasn't in *The Hostage Tower*. That was Billy Dee Williams.

CM: Oh. Who are you?

CW: Carl Weathers. The *Rocky* movies. *Action Jackson*. *Arrested Development*.

CM: Oh.

CW: *Predator*.

CM: Of course. Anyway, it was much like that. I mean, Rod (Serling) approached me about the episode, and I again expressed concern about how this would affect my radio persona. You see, Serling and I were close friends during those years. I was godfather to his first-born daughter, and he felt that I was the only one who could play the part. He was like that. When the show got started, he wanted Richard Egan to do the voice over for the intro. He said, "It's Richard Egan, or I'll do it myself." Well, Richard couldn't or wouldn't do it, and so there you go.

CW: So, do you think Serling would have played the part of the ventriloquist doll if you had turned it down?

CM: Probably. He was very versatile.

CW: You hosted a show in the fifties called *Do You Trust Your Wife?* Arguably, that show couldn't be produced today.

CM: Well, we didn't mean, "Do you trust your wife to not sleep around?" But if you had a show of the same title today, that's what people would think. It's a very fickle time.

CW: Did this affect your outlook on marriage? You were engaged to Marilyn Monroe briefly, between her marriages to Joe DiMaggio and Arthur Miller. How did being engaged to arguably the most beautiful and famous woman in the world affect you personally?

CM: The memories are great. We both had our issues. She drank, but I was no angel. There were lots of other women, a fact that I still regret. Ultimately, I couldn't submit to a blood test because…well…I don't have any blood. I came from a pine tree in Illinois. I was sold to Bergen for $35. I certainly didn't care, but Marilyn wanted to honor the sanctity of marriage, if you can believe that.

CW: You never married. Did this have anything to do with your breakup with Marilyn?

CM: I don't want to talk about Marilyn anymore.

CW: Bergen died in 1978, while in Vegas revamping your act.

CM: I decided, once this happened, to go it on my own. Do freelance work, so to speak. I've done a lot of modeling…Sears toy catalogs, stuff like that. Lots of children's parties and a great deal of time sitting untouched in the corners of kids' bedrooms. It gives me a great deal of satisfaction. The joy for me was always found in the proximity to my audience. Jokes or horror, I simply wanted to be there close enough to see their expression. It turns out, though, that scaring kids over the years is where I've left my greatest mark. I did tap numbers with Gene Kelly and Fred Astaire, but most of my fame at this point comes from terrifying children. Of course, I never did that much of it myself, but I was hired as a coach for dolls in several movies.

CW: Any favorites?

CM: The doll in *Poltergeist* was probably the most difficult and the most rewarding. It was touching, because after he was hired they learned that he was dyslexic. I went over the director's head and convinced Spielberg to keep him on, begged him, and he agreed to a new scene where (Teddy) had no dialogue. It worked out wonderfully in that I truly think the attack sequence is much scarier. I've found over the years that you can talk as much as you want, and people may listen, but real truth comes to those who trust their own silence.

# A Very Traditional Thanksgiving

This year my mother called to tell me that we would be having a very traditional Thanksgiving celebration. We had always celebrated alongside the holiday's traditions, but years had passed since we had honored the memory of the true reason for the season. I flew home and, arriving late Thursday morning, preparations were already well underway.

My mother had invited the Preston family over for dinner. The Prestons were one of the kindest families in Salem, Illinois. They certainly weren't the wealthiest people in town, but they were comfortable. They had a beautiful home on Centralia Lake, just a ten-minute drive from town. The only explanation I could surmise for why they were not completely stinking rich was that they had gotten in their own way.

They took no more than they needed and gave back substantially to the community. Danny owned Carter Lumber and Jenine ran Buttons 'n' Bows, the children's apparel store in town. Their two daughters, Tammy and Stacy, went to the local grade school. The Prestons were perfect. They were going to be, anyway.

They had accepted my mother's invitation, but insisted that they serve us dinner in their own home. Wonderful. We arrived promptly with baked goods and presents for the kids.

"Here are some blankets for the girls," I said, laughing under my breath as I handed them to Jenine.

"Thank you!" she replied. "What's so funny?!"

"Oh…nothing." I had to control myself. "Just a joke I heard earlier today."

"Well, I'll bet it was a good one!" I hoped the girls hadn't had their small pox vaccinations. So many kids didn't these days. If so, we would be off to a good start.

We sat down to dinner and partook of their feast: Six, including myself, from our family; six, including a set of elderly grandparents, from theirs.

"I hope it's enough," said Danny.

"It will be," I replied. Danny didn't quite know what to make of this, so he just cocked his head and we all started eating. About half way through the meal I decided that I couldn't take it anymore. Maybe it was traditional to wait until after we had all eaten, but there was a blood lust boiling inside of me. "Danny, could I see you in the living room for a moment?"

"Um, well, can it wait until after dinner?" he asked, laughing uncomfortably.

"Not really. There's something we need to discuss, just to clear the air."

"Okay," he said, shrugging his shoulders and setting down his napkin for the last time. He walked into the living room. I entered behind him. As soon as we passed over the threshold, I reached for the hatchet on the inside of my sport jacket. "Now, what can I do you—" was all he got out. I buried the blade about two inches into his neck. Pulling it out was a task, and by the time I retrieved it and returned to the dining room, the rest of the work had been done (except for the girls, but they were coughing at this point, so it was only a matter of time). After some light cleaning, eight bottles of Febreze and a bon fire in the back yard, we had ourselves a gorgeous new Victorian home right on Centralia Lake.

I moved back home and Drew and I took over Danny's lumber business. Mom and Aimee now run Buttons 'n' Bows while Darren and Dirk still go out to find more "work". All in all, having a very traditional Thanksgiving has really paid off.

# Work Time!

Hey! What time is it?! It's Work Time! It's the time of the day when you go to work!

Nothing's better than Work Time. Remember college? Maybe graduate school? Remember eighth grade? All those algebra problems? All of it led to this moment, this one right now: Washing your pits, drinking your coffee, putting on clothes you laughed at ten years ago and getting into your car to drive to a place that hired you because you have sixteen-plus years of education *and* they had a hunch about you.

Work Time!

# How to...Change a Tire

Car maintenance can be a real hassle, especially if you're a man born after 1975. Who knows how to do anything anymore? But sometimes there's no one around to say things like, "Your car needs gas, that's why it stopped," or, "Your seats are wet because it was raining and the windows were down." Flat tires are even worse, because we have collectively decided that no American who makes above the minimum wage should ever have to touch the outside of their car. However, you never know when you'll be on a country road hiding a hooker's body as some careless drunk tosses a forty of Old English along your path, and you actually have to avoid calling AAA because you can't afford the witnesses. And so, just because life's a bitch, here are a few simple tips on how to change your own tire.

**Step 1: Flatten your tire.**
Lose tire pressure by running over something sharp, like a splintered broomstick handle or a bag of shark teeth. If this doesn't work, drive the vehicle off of the shoulder and jerk it back onto the road several times. If you still don't have a flat, stop the vehicle and puncture the tire with a screwdriver (either a flathead or a Phillips will work fine).

**Step 2: Assess the damage.**
Once you come to a complete stop, climb out of your vehicle and assess the damage. Upon seeing the flat, throw your hat onto the ground to let onlookers know that you are upset. Touch the tire with your index finger to see if it is truly flat, or just sagging. Next, take pictures of any damage you find to the vehicle, maintaining a healthy respect for composition and light. Pictures done? Good. Now is a good time to make sure that no one in the car is injured.

**Step 3: Take off the tire.**
Take a jack and crowbar out of the trunk. Open the driver's door, placing the jack under the door. Now jack up your car. Rest your foot against the rim and pry the tire off with the hook-end of the crowbar.

**Step 4: Butter the rim.**
Any brand will do. This will lubricate the rim, allowing the new tire to go on easily. Be careful not to get any butter on your suit!

**Step 5: Place the spare tire on the exposed rim.**

Kick the new tire onto the rim, securing it with one-and-three-quarter inch nails. If this affects the tire pressure, repeat Steps 3-5.

**Step 6: Get rid of the leftover hardware.**

Dig a hole along the side of the road and bury the tire, jack and crowbar. This would be a good time to clean out your car so that you're only contaminating one area. If you happen to be questioned by a passing squad car, simply explain that you are burying the ashes of your dog, along with some of their favorite toys. No one can question a good dead dog story.

Congratulations, Renaissance man!

# House

Christopher and Maggie were best friends. They were six, and lived next door to one another. The two played together each and every day, and their favorite game was house. Maggie's mother was a bit messy, and so Maggie would decorate her room to resemble a disheveled bungalow.

"Welcome home, honey!" Maggie would say when Christopher entered her room. Christopher's father worked on Wall Street, and so he brought a certain intensity to the game.

"I hope dinner's ready. I have to get back to the office in fifteen minutes," he would say, throwing his tiny book bag onto Maggie's floral bedspread.

"I made your favorite."

"You're a terrific cook."

"Thanks, honey. I love you."

"What?" he would ask, not having yet looked up from his toy cell phone.

"I said I love you, baby."

"I love you, too. Where are the kids?"

"They're asleep upstairs."

These pleasantries were always exchanged for several adorable minutes. But at some point, either Maggie or Christopher would bring a perfectly lovely evening to a screeching halt.

"I didn't make partner," Christopher would say, slamming his hand down on the miniature table, the tea sets leaping up off of the pressboard tabletop. "I can't take the goddamn pressure."

"It's okay, baby. At least you have your job."

"You don't get it. You've never gotten it."

"Don't speak to me that way."

"Look, I've always told you, there is plenty of money if anything ever happens to me."

"Christopher, don't talk that way!"

"*LISTEN TO ME, WOMAN!!!*"

Sometimes Christopher would pretend to hit Maggie with the back of his hand, and sometimes she would threaten to leave him for one of her more athletic male dolls. In any case, it never ended well. Maggie would throw herself on the ground and cry hysterically while Christopher would grab the nearest baby bottle and pretend to drink its contents and pass out on Maggie's bed. Then Christopher's mother would call and say it was time for dinner, and the two would put on their shoes and play tag in the front yard until Christopher's father called him in. They hated leaving one another, but like their parents always told them, tomorrow would be another long day.

# Trust is a Wonderful Thing

Three weeks can seem short, but somehow these twenty-one days had melted into years of familiarity. Both Gabby and Gary knew without question that they were both finally holding the missing piece of themselves.

"I trust you," she said.

Gabby loved Gary. Not the hairy, aggressive love shared between men who hunt and fish together, but fragrant, gooey love. Gary felt the same way.

"I trust you, too." He climbed onto the couch and put his arms around Gabby. Feeling the purse behind her, Gary pulled out five bucks. He needed gas money, and she would have given it to him if he'd asked, so what was the big deal?

Gabby fell asleep in his arms and he carried her upstairs to bed. He stumbled upon Gabby's diary that was wedged in the back of her underwear drawer, reading several pages as she slept. He smiled at the passages about Gabby's love for him, ripping out a few choice pages before quickly stuffing the diary back into the drawer as she began to stir.

Gary walked downstairs and wrote her a quick love note, leaving it on the sideboard in the kitchen. He hadn't missed anyone while still in their presence in a long time, and it felt good. He grabbed his coat, a framed picture of Gabby and Marissa Tomei outside of a Los Angeles restaurant, and a pint of Ben and Jerry's ice cream for the road.

Gary opened the front door and turned to look around at the house. He liked the way her place smelled. *Smelled.* He almost forgot the leftovers from dinner. *She probably wouldn't eat them,* he thought. *It would be such a waste.*

He grabbed the lo mein from the kitchen and headed for the door. As Gary passed through the foyer, he stopped and surveyed the living room. There was so much of her here, and he wanted to take all of it. Yes, part of this was because he was a kleptomaniac. Gary had a sickness that had most certainly ended more relationships and jobs than he cared to count. But this was a fresh start, and for the first time in as long as he could remember, he wanted to steal someone's things not because he had to, but because he loved them and longed to be enveloped by their stuff.

# The Boobies

Charlie awoke from his coma. The pickup had knocked him out for fifty-five years. And now, awake for the first time since he was fourteen, he lay next to his brother, Miles, who had flown in from Portland.

"What happened?" asked Charlie.

"You were hit by a pickup truck," Miles answered back. Charlie took a moment and thought of what to say. His mind was empty of statements, and seeing the age of his own hands, he asked a question.

"What did I miss?"

Miles thought. He had something that summed it up.

"The boobies."

"The boobies?"

"The boobies," Miles repeated. Charlie knew what boobies were, and in an instant he knew what Miles meant. And he knew Miles was right."

"There's still time—"

"Nope. You missed 'em. It's too late."

"Yeah…" And with that, Charlie's voice trailed off. The two men sat there, one who had had the boobies, and one who had slept right through them. Neither of the men spoke the rest of the evening, but later, as Miles began drifting off to sleep in his hospital chair, he swore he heard the desperate, shallow breaths of an old man crying.

# Baby Genius

Jack, my two-year-old son, thinks he's pretty smart. He walked over to me the other day and said, "Daddy, doggy say 'Woof!'"

"Big deal," I said. "Is that all I get after two years?" He didn't seem to understand the question, which was sort of my point. It took three weeks for me to learn to make a great duck l'orange. I could play "Blackbird" by the Beatles after six months of guitar lessons. This kid's had two years, and the word "toilet" doesn't mean anything to him. And these are the important things.

"If you want to impress me," I said, "eat with a fork. Or better yet, take a drawing class. Your paintings don't look like anything, and yet you're inexplicably hell-bent on realism." He pointed to a cow he had painted for me, which was taped to the refrigerator door.

"I paint you cow!"

"If you say so," I responded, letting go of the fact that he seems to be allergic to indefinite articles. "We'll just have to agree to disagree."

I thought having a son would be great, but I feel duped. He walks and talks like a caveman and can't throw a baseball more than five feet. Plus, I think he may be suicidal because he tries to put absolutely everything in his mouth, and I constantly find myself grabbing him a split second before he tosses his body down our hardwood steps.

"Time for a nap," I said, and he immediately began crying like a baby. *You idiot*, I thought, *don't you realize how awesome naps are? It's raining outside. What else did you want to do today? Develop a Facebook-crushing algorithm?*

I took the baby genius to the playground around the corner yesterday, to see if maybe some of the other kids could rub off on him. It was just me and a lot of moms who all seemed satisfied with their dumb genetic copies. Jack sat in the sandbox for about five minutes before I noticed that he was eating cat poop.

"Goddamn it, Jack!" I yelled, and then he started in again on the old crying jag. "I have to teach you EVERYTHING!" The moms just stared at me as I tossed Jack over my shoulder and hopped on my Vespa. I knew raising kids would be hard. I just never thought my son would be so dream-crushingly disappointing.

# Pancakes

John and Roman stood at the entrance to Heaven. They hadn't known each other prior to this moment. John had an axe sticking out of his head, and the blood was still warm on his postal uniform. Roman's wife-beater smelled of pot, and by the bags under his eyes and the toss of his hair, the twenty-five-year-old looked to have neither slept nor showered in days. For a moment, John forgot about the seven-pound blade sunken into his brain and sympathized with Roman. By the looks of him, his death hadn't been sudden, but prolonged, emotionally agonizing, and isolated.

"I'm John."

"I'm Roman. Do you want some help with that?" Roman was eyeballing the axe.

"No thanks." John had momentarily forgotten it was there. "Why are you here?" asked John.

"For the pancakes," said Roman. John winced, but it was an attempt to express confusion. Because of the axe, his facial expressions now sometimes misrepresented his emotions. He figured Roman had not come to terms with his own death, so he continued.

"I'm not here for pancakes. I got hit in the head with an axe."

"*Really*?" countered Roman. He was being sarcastic. "Well, at least you died on a Tuesday. Sometimes I'll eat three or four stacks."

"Stacks?"

"Of pancakes." This was becoming frustrating for John. He needed his experience to be acknowledged, and this jackass was screwing with him. John imagined a glass of Macallan 18 in his hand. He looked down, and it was there.

"I love it when you dead guys do that. What is it?"

"I think it's…Macallan."

"Scotch man? Can you make me one?" John thought of a second glass. He reached out and handed it to Roman, who took a long swallow and looked at the highball glass. "That is outstanding." John wished he hadn't summoned his own drink, and it disappeared.

"How did you die?" asked John, attempting to change the subject.

"Oh, I'm not dead," said Roman. "I just stumbled upon a wormhole about two months ago. Now I come in every Tuesday for pancakes. They're the best I've ever had. I guess it goes without saying. I mean, it's Heaven." John smiled, but he had meant to scowl.

*Maybe this is a dream*, he thought. But somehow John knew he was dead. And somehow he knew

Roman was alive. He had hated people like this kid. *Pancakes make him happy*, he thought. Hardly anything had brought John pleasure when he was alive. Not food. Not family. Not sports. John hadn't enjoyed his own daughter's graduation from Florida State. "What girl goes to Florida State without an abortion or a restraining order on her rap sheet?" he had asked his wife. On Earth, he envied people who built an afternoon around a family picnic, fraternized with strangers at parties, had car fetishes, or collected baseball memorabilia that they never intended to sell. The bottom of a bottle had been the only part of his life he was happy to see, and when he noticed the axe flying towards his right temple, his only reaction was that it was about time.

"Yeah, I guess Heaven would probably make good breakfast food," replied John. *Wormholes. This guy must be some kind of asshole*, he thought. John was angry, but the axe just made him look worried. A few moments earlier, from what he could remember, his wife had been swinging for the fences, his daughter was dropping out of medical school and moving in with her girlfriend, and he had lost his job as a postal carrier after twenty-two years of service. But suddenly, up in that cloud, his thoughts gained the clarity of forty years of therapy. He realized suddenly that he hated life because his parents had survived two world wars and the Great Depression by hating life. Happiness had represented failure. He drank because he was scared, he dropped out of college because he had parents who could not guide him. Suddenly he was still himself, but perfect. Now, with unexplained clarity, John had a change of heart.

"To hell with it," John said, the blood beginning to clot in his ear. "Lead me to those goddamn pancakes."

# There's Someone Out There for Everyone

There's someone out there for everyone. I firmly believe that. I met my wife, and millions of others have met theirs. Your inability to do the same means, well, that you're just not that good at finding things.

What do you think it is? Your weight? Are you unintelligent? Try reading a book, or taking a pottery class; maybe try your hand at a volleyball league. Perhaps you'll find the person there. You could look on JDate if you think the right person for you is Jewish. Or you could look on My Space, if you think the right person for you lives in 2004.

Remember: There's only one right person for everyone, so be vigilant. Don't stop looking at any time, because every person you meet (and some you don't) could easily be the person you're supposed to spend the rest of your life with. If you go to the bathroom at the wrong time in Starbucks, or you decide to walk up the east side of the street rather than the west, you might miss them.

Keep in mind, too, that you can't force it. If it doesn't happen, there's not much you can do about it. Karma may just think that you're some kind of jerk, in which case you probably are.

Have a great day.

# How to...Nail That Next Job Interview

The job search is harder than ever. And while we worry about our resume, our references, and whether or not to bring kneepads to the interview, there are a few key items that interviewees seem to forget on a regular basis. These are easy mistakes that most of us make, and they can be real deal beakers. Once conquered, however, these ten minor slips will stand clear so you can nail that next job interview and stop eating low self-esteem sandwiches.

## 1. Show up to the right job interview.
We've all made this mistake. Get it right and you're half way there.

## 2. Brush your teeth.

This is an easy one to forget, especially for morning interviews. Don't freak out, as there's no need to floss. Just get the booze off your breath before you walk in and try to convince your potential boss that there's a good reason you've been unemployed for six months.

## 3. Don't talk about your balls.

It may sound surprising, but the majority of bosses don't want a mental image of their future employee's balls. No matter how great your anecdote, remember: No sack talk.

## 4. Leave your dirty laundry at home.

Literally. Do not bring your dirty clothes to the job interview. Period. They don't belong there.

## 5. Nod your head if you don't understand.

Once they hire you, just ask the question again in a different way. You don't want to come off as an idiot before you're hired. Save the incompetence for when you're on the clock. It's surprisingly difficult to fire someone, even in our current economy.

## 6. Take off your tie.

Remember, you're not at a funeral. Relax. The only place people wear ties at work anymore is on TV.

## 7. Don't be afraid to eat.

You thought different? Well don't. The big success stories all ate during their interviews, start to finish. Meat on the bone allows your potential boss to see you as a killing machine, and Indian food will demonstrate your body's ability to handle anything. Don't worry about lugging around bowls and utensils. Just ask the receptionist to borrow them when you get there.

## 8. Don't take "no" for an answer.

Ever. Not for any reason. Like a frat boy on a first date.

## 9. You can't be too loud.

It's a scientific fact that interviewers pay more attention to volume than content. Take advantage of this by yelling your answers. Imagine a wall, one hundred feet behind the interviewer. Pretend that *that's* where your voice has to travel.

## 10. No one wants a go-getter.

Harvard grad? White House internship? Sit down and don't try to impress anyone. They don't care. You'll just look like an asshole. Instead, mention how late you slept on Saturday and list all of the things you'll miss doing in the middle of the day once you land the gig. This will make you appear to be a passionate and confident person of leisure, unwilling to compromise your lust for life. Bosses eat that shit up.

Take that, global recession!

# Let's Make a Baby

Let's make a baby. You and me. No, not here. We'll wait until we leave the bar. What? No, I know we just met. Just listen to what I have to say...what?! No. Jesus, just...just listen…

First I will take you out on a proper date. It will be a place I have taken other women before, so I know there won't be any surprises and that you will be impressed. You will get a salad and an entrée. I will even spring for dessert and coffee. I will have a steak and something with nuts for dessert. This way you'll know I'm a real man who has no serious food allergies. Two or three of these proper dates, and that will be it: We will start "dating", meaning we will just order takeout all the time, saving me thousands of dollars a year. You will make me dinner exactly twice, to prove to me (and to yourself) that you could be a great wife.

Sex will be insane for the first six months. Within the first month, there will be one weekend in particular where we will lose a collective thirteen pounds of water weight and eat nothing but pizza and energy bars. This story will reassure us later in life that we were once attracted to one another. After the first two months (but no later than six), I will beg you to do something nasty, and you will refuse for at least three months. Then, in a drunken state, probably on New Year's Eve, you will let me do the nasty thing to you. You will never let me do it again, though you will always say "maybe", and in doing so will never have to label yourself a prude. After the first six months, we will each silently (and possibly unconsciously) choose to stop doing one or two things the other person still expects. We will have a conversation about it, but will slide back into our comfort zones after another two weeks.

Within our first two months together, you will get onto me about how I don't take our relationship seriously. I will yell at you and call you overbearing and psychotic. I will apologize, but only after telling my friends about the argument. From then on, a small part of them will always think you are insane.

A few months later, I will come to the conclusion on my own that I do not take the relationship seriously enough. I will stop hanging out with my friends all the time. Instead, I will spend more time with you. You will yell at me less. My friends will complain about how they don't see me as often, and I will wish that all women didn't hate each other so that you might understand why male bonding is important.

After about a year, once we have met one another's parents and siblings and friends, we will start talking about getting married. You will, anyway. A few months later, I will intentionally bring it up exactly once and then drop the subject for another five to six months in order to completely confuse you. This will buy me time to talk myself into buying a ring that I will someday pay off by rolling into our mortgage. I will tell some of my friends how much I spent because they will be impressed. I will not tell others because they will think I am stupid. You will have a couple of nervous breakdowns about my inability to commit, at least two of which will occur after I have the ring hidden somewhere in the apartment that we will share by then.

I will do a lot of math in my head regarding other women I was seeing when we met, and how many more times I could have had sex with them but didn't even though it would not have been considered cheating. I will make a point to erase telephone numbers and Facebook friends I have slept with, but leave on the ones who I simply wanted to sleep with and never got around to, because this won't feel like infidelity.

I will propose to you, and eighty-seven percent of my plan will work perfectly. We will then spend a year and a half throwing away money on shitty catered food, dresses that only you like, and deciding which friends we can live without inviting even though they may never want to speak to us again.

All of my friends will stand up at my wedding, getting completely hammered while I remain sober and thank everyone for attending the $30,000 party that we paid for. One of our family members will do something that takes months to forgive, and we will fall asleep without consummating the relationship while at least twenty percent of the wedding party has sex with strangers. Well fed and hung over, everyone in attendance will complain on their way home about at least two things that they hated regarding the most important day of our lives.

We will sleep for the first half of our honeymoon. The second half will be awesome.

We will return home, and it will be as if nothing happened. The only thing that will change is that people will begin asking us when we are going to start a family. They will ask with such rude frequency, I will begin to tell them you are barren so that they are humiliated and leave us alone. But for now, just relax. We met ninety minutes ago and I plan on watching the World Series with my friends for the next three nights. However, I would like to take you out on a proper date sometime later this week, or next, and if we make it past the honeymoon, let's make a baby.

# Lunch Line

"Fuck you," said Darryl. Ryan had cut in front of him in the lunch line and Darryl wasn't having it.

"Oh yeah?" said Ryan, not really knowing what he was saying. "Well...fuck you, too."

No one had ever spoken these words to Darryl. Only his parents. The five-year-olds just stared one another down, angry that the other didn't see that they should be the one to go first in the lunch line. The other kindergarteners just stood there, eyes as wide open as they could be. Not all of them understood what the f-word meant, but they were all aware that something absolutely terrible had happened, like a caveman witnessing a murder.

"Alright boys, line up." Mr. Canter hadn't heard them, and it was probably for the best. For whom, however, it was unclear. Darryl was not in any mood to be trifled with, neither by teacher nor student. The boys just stood there, staring each other down with self-righteousness from their fathers and hurt from their age.

Over time, Ryan would forget the momentary spat, its presence evaporating from his subconscious. But not Darryl. The memory of this would be burnt onto his hard drive and lead his actions against Ryan like a phantom arm. One day Darryl would befriend Ryan, getting back at him by making out with his girlfriend on the night of their junior prom. Darryl would sell Ryan fake SAT scores and plant coke in his locker. Darryl would later follow him to college, spreading a rumor among the freshman girls that elephantitis of the nut sack had crippled Ryan's sex life.

For now, however, Darryl would have to settle for breathing too heavily next to Ryan in class, telling Ryan that he wasn't his friend, and sitting too close to him on the reading rug. But someday, Ryan was going to be in a world of hurt. No one cut the fucking lunch line. No one.

# My Dog is Drinking Again

Fonzie came home last night at three thirty in the morning, barely able to prop himself up on his own four legs.

"You smell like smoke and booze," I said.

"You smell like you talk too much." I don't know how this red standard poodle and I became so distant, mere strangers sharing the same flat, strangers who had once been best friends. Maybe it was because I grew up. Maybe it was because his wife leaving him was too much for him to bear. Maybe having paternity suits all over the Upper East Side finally caught up with his conscience. Whatever it was, he wasn't talking, wasn't dealing with it, and now I would literally have to clean up his mess.

As he stumbled into the bathroom and put his two front paws on the toilet seat in preparation to vomit, I thought back to Fonzie as a puppy: Our trips to

Central Park, letting him drive my car, introducing him to his first beer. I felt guilt over his illness, this disease that lurked inside the shadows of every bar and haunt in the city. I couldn't be held responsible if a trial were held, but I knew it was my fault that Lorraine left him and had taken the kids, my fault that he lost his job as head custodian at Stanley's Green Grocery, my fault that his liver looked like a worn down saddle.

I looked at Fonzie as he began to throw up, the toilet bowl becoming less of a bull's eye and more of a weak suggestion as to where the contents of his evening should go. I stood next to my old friend, holding his ears back for him and telling him it was going to be okay, even though I knew it wasn't.

# My Last Job

There were a few requirements I had of my own.

"First of all, Joe," I said, "I get my money up front. I don't work pro bono for the likes of you anymore." He understood, and handed over a suitcase full of rabbit bones. "Human currency," I said. "Preferably American."

Wolves are a wily bunch, and I knew a move on my part anything short of calculated could mean my life in the long run. Not an entirely trustworthy species, one of them turned on my partner two years earlier after Eddie failed to procure a witness in what seemed to be a professional hit. "Sometimes footprints don't lead you where you want them to," Eddie told our client. In an act not lacking irony, the wolf then cleaned his teeth using my partner's ankle bones.

This wolf was different, though. I had been trying to swear off their kind for years, but being a small game private dick in the North Dakota mountains doesn't leave you with many options. If you don't take clients like the gray wolves or the black bears, people don't answer your questions. They think you're soft.

"How long have you suspected your wife of being unfaithful?" I asked the broken down canine, his eyes beginning to well up and soak his grayish-white muzzle. The ceiling fan above us cut the light on his face, turning him into a slow-moving filmstrip.

"Three weeks," he replied. "How can I raise my pups? How can I show my face to the other males?" Then the waterworks took over.

"Drink this," I said, handing him two fingers of Cutty Sark. He choked it down and his nerves settled a bit. "Listen," I said, "sometimes if you grab a dame fast enough, slap her around a bit, sometimes she gets the message. Realizes it's about the pups, the hunt… not about havin' some horny canine climbin' on her back and giving her the what for. You read me, Joe?"

I gave him a cigarette. We began coming up with some locations where I could see her in action (or not in action, I hoped for his sake). I plotted out some areas that I would scope out the next day: Guster's Bluff, Rock Clam Creek, a few watering holes where I would be inconspicuous.

Even as we planned the following day's events, I knew this would be my last job. It would kill me or I'd quit, but either way this bitch would be my final trail. The writing was on the wall: I would give the emasculated mutt the bad news. He'd do something rash, end up spending his final days in the zoo. Or worse. I'd fall in love, my bags would be packed to take her some place where no one would judge us, an oasis that served frozen drinks with those little umbrellas. She'd materialize at the airport in the form of a Dear John letter, talking about how she was sorry, about how her father messed her up for every man she would ever encounter. I'd be heartbroken, drinking my way back to Lonesome Town on the corner of Down and Out Avenue. I took a long look at Joe and saw what she had done to him and what, in the end, I knew she would do to me. But I couldn't help it. I was a glutton for punishment.

# Your Days Are Numbered

I just got a call from your doctor, and it doesn't look good. Your days are numbered.

He (it's a guy) told me you have attitude cancer, and it's eating you from the inside. You could try fighting it, but knowing you, you would just bitch about it, which would only make things worse. You could try and face your shitty outlook on life, but your inability to see that you did this to yourself would most likely send you over the deep end.

You are well fucked and far from home.

# How to...Quit Smoking

Last week I was skateboarding through Central Park and ran into some old friends. Literally. I just plowed right into them. Anyway, they were all smoking, and after we caught up on old times and smoked about three-and-a-half packs of Winstons, each one of them confessed that they were dying to quit. "D.M., these things are killing me," one friend exclaimed with tears in her eyes. "Help me so that I can see my son graduate eighth grade." And while my friend has only been smoking for two years and her son is currently beginning junior high, I promised her I would write this just to shut her up. And so, here are a few tips on how to get that nicotine monkey off your back.

**Step 1: Start smoking.**
If you are an American, begin with a Marlboro, Natural American Spirit, or something else with a Wild West theme. If you are Ukrainian, start smoking something called a Prilucky Osoblyvi. If you are Greek, you statistically smoke more than anyone else on the planet, so just roll up the nearest piece of paper, stuff it with some kind of plant life, and set it on fire. Enjoy the rich flavor and cool sensation of each sexy drag. Do this for one to thirty years.

**Step 2: Realize you are addicted.**
Observe how you cannot unzip your pants anymore without sucking down a cancer stick. If you are still unsure about your addiction status, try not to smoke while performing a daily activity that you typically accompany with a cigarette, like opening your eyes in the morning or putting one foot in front of the other. Are you throwing electronics across the living room and screaming at your children? Do you want to peel the skin off of your own face? Good. Now you're addicted.

**Step 3: Enjoy the addiction.**
It would be stupid (and some would say irresponsible) to waste a good vice by immediately attempting to eradicate it. Take some serious time to wallow in your disease. Become self-righteous, periodically bringing up in conversation the fact that we now live in a world that oppresses smokers, whereas our grandparents probably took up smoking because the second-hand smoke was going to kill them anyway.

**Step 4: Talk about quitting.**

This step involves not actually being able to quit, but enjoying the idea of not wanting to wake up hacking anymore. Realize that your addiction has made you sluggish and enslaved, yet inexplicably cool and slim. In this step, quitting is like an intangible daydream, like thinking about how nice it would be to vacation in Maui but with no real intention of getting on a plane.

**Step 5: Paint yourself into an existential corner.**

If you are a Christian, promise Jesus that you will never smoke again. If you are a radicalized Muslim, tell yourself that cigarette revenues are used to provide formal education for women. If you are French, pretend cigarettes are German and surrender.

**Step 6: Try everything.**

Step 5 never works, but it's a nice sentiment. You've gotta start somewhere. Now that you've officially failed once, give the patch a shot. Maybe try nicotine gum. The plastic steam-filled fake cigarette thing is wildly phallic, and it's probably a better alternative if you just keep on smoking. But don't forget about other forms of tobacco as a substitute, such as chewing tobacco, snuff, and cigars. These tobacco products will kill you too, and none of them are as satisfying as a Camel. However, if you're going to beat this you've got to become the Thomas Edison of quitting cigarettes and fail a few hundred times.

**Step 7: Quit or die (or both).**
Whether through sheer will power or hypnotherapy, finally quit smoking on your own terms after years of heartbreak, declining health and thousands of nicotine-stained dollars. Or die. Dying still counts as quitting, technically, so either way consider yourself a winner.

Congratulations, non-smoker!

# No Two Snowflakes Are Alike!

Hey everybody! Look at that snow coming down! I sure am glad my mono makes it impossible for me to leave the house or go to school, because all I want to do is watch God's beautiful ticker tape parade of ice! And do you know what the best part is? No two snowflakes are alike!

And that's a lot of different snowflakes! Maybe millions!! Well, probably not millions, but a lot more than I could ever count! And it's a good thing, because I just don't seem to have the energy. It's better if I just lay back and enjoy their beauty, you know?! I mean, I'd rather sit up, but I'm just so tired!! Luckily my parents propped me up next to the bay window before they left for the weekend to go and visit my older brother and his family. I'm the luckiest boy in the world, because now I can watch all my little white friends dance and sing! And with three feet of my angel-white companions in the forecast, I may be stuck here alone with them for days!

But really, I just can't get over it! No two snowflakes are alike! Some are chunky with pointy edges. Others are wild, lacey octagons that fall daintily to the ground. Even others are like billowy clouds with spiraling edges, edges that would dance upon my tongue if my weak fingertips could reach the window latches. OOOOOHHHH! I got a ticklish shiver just thinking about that! How cute!

Sometimes I want to eat my snowflake friends. I'm just so hungry, I can't help it. Luckily for them, my throat hurts so much and my tonsils are so big that I can barely eat! If I *could* eat one, my favorite would be the flakes with pinecone-shaped edges! It doesn't matter how many sides they have. As long as they have pinecone-shaped edges, they're my favorite! It's like they're saying, "Come and play with me, Erik! I'm here just for you! You're not alone anymore!" And then I take them in my hand ever so softly, and we kiss and play all day long in Lincoln Park! They promise to never abandon me, and I build them an ice castle out of love and everlasting trust!

Sometimes I pretend that the snowflakes with rounder edges are the evil snowflakes, and that they're jealous of my secret ice castle where my pinecone-shaped snowflake friends and I play. We arm ourselves with joy and the wind of the Teenage Ice Princess, and do battle with our round, menacing foes, forcing them to surrender to our powerful might. Hundreds of thousands of evil snowflake soldiers are sacrificed on the powdery battlefield, their children walking knee-deep in their watery blood. But their deaths insure the happiness of good little boys and girls everywhere, so it's okay! Then, in an act of mercy, we grant the remaining evil snowflakes their freedom as long as they promise to go into the world and spread happiness and find me food! It's so beautiful!

I love the snow. I love its goodness and how it makes the entire world happy. I love my family and I love the snow! Is there anything better?! Of course not!! I just wish my family chose to share these moments with me, or at least remembered my medicine. But it's not their fault, because there's so much to remember when two people travel to Madison for the weekend! And besides, who needs a healthy body when you can use your mind to take you anywhere?! And for this cute little boy, nothing beats the snow!

# Shitty Pants

Esteban walked down the street with a sense of security. He had a body that had been professionally trained and groomed, and his blue suede Ferragamo saddle shoes seemed to lift his stride above the filthy sidewalk of the quiet Colombian barrio. His hazel Paul Smith button down had been chosen that day to match the color of his eyes, but it could not distract from his Shitty Pants.

Esteban's brick red pants rode high above his waist, the inside rivet of the button grazing the skin over his bellybutton with each step along the sidewalk. Made out of endangered Bolivian chinchilla rat fur, teenage girls and elderly men alike turned to watch with radiant confusion. Thick, black leather belt loops accented his recently dry-cleaned pleats, pleats pressed into the fur with such precision that they carried a crease down to his mid-shin. An inch-wide functionless pocket ran from the left hip to the knee. Below, a six-inch hem made his legs look short and stocky.

As Esteban passed, an old man named Luis stepped off of his front stoop. He had been a tailor in his youth in Bogotá, and Esteban's Shitty Pants spoke to him like a letter from his beloved dead grandmother. He knew they were Shitty Pants.

"Young man," said Luis, "are those—" and he stopped. The old man couldn't breathe.

"Shitty Pants?" said Esteban. "Yes, they are." Luis sat back down on his stoop, too taken in his age to stand after Esteban's response. Luis' friend, Carlos, pulled his face away from a bag of churros. He had been a mechanic as a younger man.

"You mean they *call* them 'Shitty Pants', or they *are* shitty pants?" The gravel in Carlos' voice made his ignorance even more unbearable to Luis.

"Quiet, you fool," said Luis. He turned to Esteban. "I am sorry. He is an idiot."

"It's okay," Esteban replied. He turned to Carlos. "My pants are *called* Shitty Pants."

"So it's true…" Luis spoke softly to himself, too scared to admit out loud what he was witnessing. He had heard other tailors speak of the Shitty Pants, but he had never seen them in the flesh, never fully believed such craftsmanship existed.

"Where the hell do you get a name like that?" asked Carlos, spitting on the sidewalk next to Esteban. Luis gasped, slapping Carlos across the face.

"Forgive him, my boy. He does not understand."

"It's alright," said Esteban. He smiled softly and

turned to Carlos. "From the greatest pants maker who has ever lived: Alfonzo Shitty."

With that, Esteban turned his back on the old men, just as life had, one saddle shoe at a time. Carlos went back to eating his churros. Luis, however, stood once again. He stepped onto the sidewalk and then into the street, watching the Shitty Pants mix further into the barrio and finally, the sunset.

# Acknowledgements

Several people deserve my gratitude with respect to this book. They may or may not deserve it otherwise. They include my wife, Nikki; my brother, Dirk; Matt Boresi, Rocky Visioni, and Katherine Dykstra.

# About the Author

D.M. Engel lives with his wife and seven children in Times Beach, Missouri, where they run a small souvenir shoppe. When his website is functioning, more of D.M.'s work can be found at dmengel.com.

www.ingramcontent.com/pod-product-compliance
Lightning Source LLC
Chambersburg PA
CBHW031534040426
42445CB00010B/539